D1081643

Maurice Sendak

Twayne's United States Authors Series
Children's Literature

Ruth K. MacDonald, Editor

TUSAS 598

Maurice Sendak
Photo copyright © 1991 by Chris Callis

Maurice Sendak

Amy Sonheim

University of Missouri–Columbia

Twayne Publishers • New York

Maxwell Macmillan Canada • Toronto

Maxwell Macmillan International • New York   Oxford   Singapore   Sydney

741.5
S

Selection from *Where the Wild Things Are*, copyright © 1963 by Maurice Sendak. All rights reserved. Used with permission.

Selection from *In the Night Kitchen*, copyright © 1970 by Maurice Sendak. All rights reserved. Used with permission.

Selection from *Outside Over There*, copyright © 1981 by Maurice Sendak. All rights reserved. Used with permission.

Maurice Sendak
Amy Sonheim

Copyright © 1991 by Twayne Publishers

All rights reserved. No part of this book may be reproduced or transmitted in any form or by any means, electronic or mechanical, including photocopying, recording, or by any information storage and retrieval system, without permission in writing from the Publisher.

Twayne Publishers
Macmillan Publishing Company
866 Third Avenue
New York, New York 10022

Maxwell Macmillan Canada Inc.
1200 Eglinton Avenue East
Suite 200
Don Mills, Ontario M3C 3N1

10 9 8 7 6 5 4 3 2 1

The paper used in this publication meets the minimum requirements of American National Standard for Information Sciences—Permanence of Paper for Printed Library Materials, ANSI Z39.48-1984. ∞™

Printed and bound in the United States of America

Library of Congress Cataloging-in-Publication Data

Sonheim, Amy.
    Maurice Sendak / Amy Sonheim.
        p.   cm. — (Twayne's United States authors series ; TUSAS 598.
    Children's literature)
    Includes bibliographical references and index.
    ISBN 0-8057-7628-1
    1. Sendak, Maurice—Criticism and interpretation.   2. Children's stories, American—History and criticism.   3. Children's stories, American—Illustrations.   I. Title.   II. Series: Twayne's United States authors series ;
TUSAS 598.   III. Series: Twayne's United States authors series. Children's literature.
PS3569.E6Z89   1992
741.6'42'092—dc20   91-34072
                                                                              CIP

Contents

Preface

Once considered a controversial artist for children with his pictures of wild beasts and naked bodies, Maurice Sendak now holds the revered position of America's most popular picture-book author. Teachers and librarians regard Sendak's illustrated and picture books as "musts" for their students and patrons. Embraced by the public as a first-rate entertainer, Sendak is esteemed as well by the academic community as a top-of-the-line artist. The varied canon offers a veritable gold mine of art to explore.

For some reason, biographical criticism set the precedent of critical approaches to Sendak's art. Possibly the fact that Sendak came into the limelight carrying the question of the appropriateness of his work for children whetted his readers' appetites for the inside story on the man who created all the hullabaloo. A wealth of interviews with Sendak were published during the sixties and seventies, culminating in 1980 with the most comprehensive book on Sendak's art, Selma G. Lanes's picture biography *The Art of Maurice Sendak,* a colorful repository of personal anecdotes behind each artistic endeavor of Sendak.

In the eighties, the academic community began to redefine categories and genres. The notion was entertained and gradually accepted that children's literature could and should have the same privilege of close scrutiny that other fine literature received. The study of how visual images express meaning was shifting from the art history department into other departments that practiced reading pictures, symbols, and signs. The dynamics of a dual narrative between pictures and words drew attention to the picture book as a distinct genre needing a particular type of consideration. Sendak's work offered pristine territory for such analyses in detail. Consequently, the eighties witnessed a burgeoning of critical work on Sendak's art, which in turn was met by even more interviews, books, essays, and operas by Sendak.

Intrigued by Sendak's success in both the marketplace and the classroom, I wanted to explore how he made his art so engaging. Specifically, I wanted to discover the intricacies of his verbal and visual styles. In this book I examine aspects of Sendak's style that have not received much analysis—the collaborative pictorial narrative of his early illustrations, a linguistic study of the narrative in *Kenny's Window,* an examination of the emblematic images in *Higglety Pigglety Pop!,* a study of the rhythmic language in his picture-book texts, and a source study of *Dear Mili.* For such varied media, I have taken eclectic approaches—biographical, linguistic, art historical, and genre. Though I discuss Sendak's style for his texts and pictures, I have chosen to quote only the former and not to reprint the latter. The wide availability of Sendak's illustrations in their original color, dimensions and layout made their reproduction in this text needless, if not unpreferable, as well.

Much thanks to Anna-Margaret Fields who proofread tirelessly, and to Patricia Crown, Gilbert Youmans, Mary Lago, Tom Hanks, Douglas Sonheim and Liz Fowler who provided solid criticisms along the way.

Chronology

1928 Maurice Sendak born 10 June in Brooklyn, New York, the third child of Philip and Sarah Sendak.

1946 Graduates from Lafayette High School.

1947 *Atomics for Millions,* first published illustrations.

1948 Attends Art Student League for two years. Works, doing window displays, for F. A. O. Schwarz.

1950 Meets editor Ursula Nordstrom.

1951 *Wonderful Farm,* first illustrated children's book.

1952 Illustrates *A Hole Is to Dig* for Ruth Krauss.

1953 First trip to Europe.

1954 Illustrates *Wheel on the School* for Meindert DeJong; wins Newbery Medal.

1956 *Kenny's Window.*

1957 Illustrates *Little Bear* for Else Holmelund Minarik.

1960 *Nutshell Library.*

1962 Illustrates *Mr. Rabbit and the Lovely Present* for Charlotte Zolotow.

1963 *Where the Wild Things Are.*

1964 Receives Caldecott Medal for *Wild Things.* Illustrates *Bat-Poet* for Randall Jarrell.

1967 Suffers heart attack. Death of Jennie, his terrier. *Higglety Pigglety Pop!*

1968 His mother, Sarah Sendak, dies.

1970 Receives Hans Christian Andersen Award. *In the Night Kitchen.*

1973 *Juniper Tree.*

1975 Animated film *Really Rosie Starring the Nutshell Kids.*

1976 Illustrates *Fly by Night* for Randall Jarrell.

1979 *Magic Flute* premieres.

1980 Opera of *Wild Things* premieres.

1981 *Outside Over There. Cunning Little Vixen* premieres.

1982 *Love for Three Oranges* premieres.

1983 *Nutcracker* premieres.

1985 Opera of *Higglety Pigglety Pop!* premieres.

1988 *Dear Mili. Caldecott & Co.*

1990 *Idomeneo* premieres. Wins first Empire State Award for Excellence in Literature for Young People.

1

Eclectic Influences

Born in Brooklyn, New York, on 10 June 1928, Maurice Sendak entered a world of seemingly incompatible traditions. Sendak describes the contradicting influences on his life from his newly immigrated Polish-Jewish parents, Philip and Sarah ("Sadie") Sendak, and their new setting in America: "On the one hand, I lived snugly in [my parents'] old-country world, a world far from urban society where the laws and customs of a small Jewish village were scrupulously and lovingly obeyed. And on the other hand, I was bombarded with the intoxicated gush of America in that convulsed decade, the thirties."[1] Even through the eyes of his parents, Sendak saw conflicting pictures of the old country. From his mother, Sendak received an impression of Poland as a land under siege: she emphasized how her brothers and sisters were forced to hide when the Cossacks invaded their village. From his father, Sendak received an impression of Poland as a romantic playground, as Philip fondly recalled the times of "ice-skating on a lovely pond."[2] It is Sendak's openness to these and his other childhood memories—both the comforting and the frightening ones—that continually focuses his holistic vision for his work as an artist.

Sendak reminisces that his earliest encounter with "the intoxicated gush of America" was his weekly outings with Philip and

Sadie to the neighborhood cinema, the Kingsway Theater. On Friday nights, partly to appease his mother's desire for a new set of dishes, Maurice accompanied his parents to a magical night at the movies. Sadie received her bonus "depression glass," and Sendak received a magical dose of fantasy. "With their exotic, glossy fantasticalness," jokes Sendak, "[these movies] permanently dyed my imagination a silvery Hollywood color" ("Andersen," 6). In the mid-1930s Sendak saw Busby Berkeley's *Gold Diggers,* Charlie Chaplin movies, *King Kong,* and *Fantasia.* Part of the thrill for Sendak inside the dark theater was the curious, childhood delight of being scared out of his wits. He remembers "one unforgettable evening" he sat by his parents and watched *The Invisible Man,* Claude Rains himself, slowly unbandage his head to reveal a ghastly nothing.[3]

The mid-1930s were also "the golden age of Mickey" for Sendak. Though not a scary figure, as were "the pleasurably dreaded King Kong" ("Andersen," 6) and the Invisible Man, Mickey Mouse fascinated Sendak. The artist now realizes that he was attracted to Mickey because of his "bizarre proportions" and acutely sensuous nature. In a tribute to his animated hero, Sendak as an adult recollects that "the great rounded head extended still farther by those black saucer ears, the black trunk fitting snugly into ballooning red shorts, the tiny legs stuffed into delicious doughy yellow shoes. The giant white gloves, yellow buttons, pie-cut eyes, and bewitching grin were the delectable finishing touches" (*C&C,* 108). In a tongue-in-cheek apology for his early infatuation with the "wonderful world of Walt Disney," Sendak explains that had he been born in Michelangelo's day and been afforded the opportunity to live around the corner from the Sistine Chapel, he might have grown up to be a "more enlightened and tasteful human being." But because he grew up as a poor kid in Brooklyn during the depression, he "made shift" with the Kingsway Theater featuring Mickey Mouse (*C&C,* 212). Perhaps Sendak preferred it this way. He lovingly refers to Mickey Mouse and the other wonders of his childhood—Little Nemo, Krazy Kat, Charlie Chaplin, and Buster Keaton—as his "nursery school of art."[4]

In contrast to the glittery features at the cinema, most other nights were highlighted by Philip Sendak's telling of bedtime *myselles* (Yiddish for "little stories").[5] These stories had neither "happily-ever-after" endings nor pallid plots. "He would sit at the edge of the bed and tell us cliffhangers," notes Sendak. "Some of these I repeated in school and was sent home with instructions to have my mouth washed out. My father didn't censor himself or worry about what was appropriate for children. We idolized him."[6] Before his death, at the prompting of Maurice, Philip Sendak recorded pieces of these tales in Yiddish, later translated into English and titled *In Grandpa's House* (1985).[7]

Philip's tales reveal direct influences on Sendak's work in both subject and spirit. The father imparted a holistic view of life to his son. Much like a folklorist, Philip spares no terror to his protagonist, David. Along his journey, David encounters ghosts at midnight, goblins at the window, and dwarves with whips. Likewise, Sendak includes monsters, goblins, and danger in his own fantasies. Yet countering the element of fear in his book, Philip balances the stories with comfort. *Grandpa's House* is as much about David's finding a safe haven in his grandfather's home as it is about his adversaries along the way. The younger Sendak also balances the sense of anxiety in his stories with a sense of security. Max returns from the wild things to his mother's warm dinner, and Mickey returns from the frenetic bakers to his bed, tired and happy.

The elder Sendak imparted particular fantasy motifs as well. The dream motifs Philip weaves into his stories appear at times verbatim in Maurice's art. In *Grandpa's House* Philip tells how David flies through the air on a giant bird. Sendak pictures this same scenario as an embellishment to his illustrations for Ruth Krauss's *I'll Be You and You Be Me* (1954).[8] Elsewhere Maurice restages Philip's dream plot of David's becoming lost with Ida's horrible predicament of getting turned the wrong way in *Outside Over There*.[9]

In their respective approaches to art, Philip and Maurice achieve a sense of realistic truth in their fantasies by reshaping their personal experiences into stories. Philip models *Grandpa's House* on an event from his own adolescence. Growing up in Poland as a teenager, he had disobeyed his father, provoking him to place the curse of the village rabbi on his son. For a sanctuary from his father's anger, Philip ran to his grandfather's house in a neighboring village (P. Sendak, 5). In *Grandpa's House* Philip reshapes this adventure into the tale of young David, who also becomes separated from his parents; Philip resolves David's troubles by also leading him to his grandfather. As if vicariously given a second chance with his own father, Philip duly includes a penitent moral: he reminds his young reader-listeners that children should help their parents.

As early as 1934, Maurice already exhibited an imagination that sought to synthesize his parents' old world with his new one. In that year he and his 11-year-old brother, Jack, followed in their father's footsteps to create a story of their own together, their first book, entitling it *They Were Inseparable*. The story combines a strict punishment for the cultural taboo of incest with gushy passion. Throwing roses at the feet of their elder sister, Natalie, Jack and Maurice wrote about a brother and sister who were so fond of each other that they would rather die together than be separated. The story climaxes when the sister rushes to see the brother at the hospital, after he has undergone some catastrophic accident, and "the two of them just grab each other—like the conclusion of *Tosca*—and exclaim 'We are inseparable!' Everybody tries to pull them apart, but they jump out the window of the Brooklyn Jewish Hospital together" (Lanes, 13). For all the innocence and naïveté of their dramatic tale, the sons of Philip and Sadie knew it would not do to have a brother and sister fall in love, even if the young boys could not explain the situation at the time.

As much as Maurice doted on Natalie, he sometimes was deathly afraid of her. Having two overworked parents, Philip a tailor and Sadie a full-time homemaker, Maurice was often foisted off on teenage Natalie to be baby-sat. Sendak recalls her "demonic rages" at this injustice. Worse yet, in 1939 Natalie lost him in the crowd at the New York World's Fair (*C&C*, 209). Getting separated from Natalie in the crowd made such an impression on Sendak as a child that he later used this memory as the impetus for *In the Night Kitchen.*[10] He remembers finding "himself alone in the 'Uneeda Biscuit' exhibit, where the motto was 'We Bake While You Sleep.'"[11] Later he would write about Mickey aroused from his sleep to avoid being baked alive by the cooks in the night kitchen.

Throughout the years of the Great Depression and following, Sendak felt loved and happy living with his father, mother, older sister, and brother. But he felt completely otherwise about the relatives who visited on Sundays. He resented their pinching his cheeks and eating his family's food. "And I hated the fact that my mother was a very slow cooker," says Sendak, because "we had to spend what seemed like hours in the living room with people we detested" (*C&C,* 214). Sendak survived these grueling afternoons by studying the faces of his relatives. He made "note of every mole, every bloodshot eye, every hair curling out of every nostril, every blackened tooth" (*C&C,* 214). These Sunday relatives became the ancestors of Sendak's wild things, serving as their grotesque models (Shirk, 1).

As much as Sendak loved home, he hated school. He hated being crowded by other children, he hated vying for status, and most of all he hated the stifling effect school had on his creativity (Lanes, 22). One way school suppressed Sendak's artistic instinct was by condemning what he loved, specifically Walt Disney. Sendak explains, "I was told that [Disney] corrupted the fairy tale and that he was the personification of poor taste. I began to suspect my own instinctual response to Mickey. It took me nearly twenty years to rediscover the pleasure of that first response and to fuse it with my own work as an artist. It took me just as long to forget the corrupting effect of school" (*C&C,* 108).

During his time at Lafayette High School, Sendak, though mediocre in other subjects, excelled in art. His art teacher gave him the freedom to do as he pleased, and Sendak's talent blossomed. He regularly contributed a comic strip to the school newspaper and did drawings for both the yearbook and the school literary magazine (Lanes, 23). By his senior year in 1945, Sendak had become "something of a celebrity at Lafayette." It was through his senior physics teacher, Hyman Ruchlis, that Sendak landed his first professional job as an illustrator: he was paid $100 to draw black-and-white sketches for a textbook entitled *Atomics for the Millions.* Even in this book's pedagogic format, Sendak incorporated his ability to animate pictures, as if setting them to music. He illustrated the bonding of sodium and chloride atoms into molecules, for example, as individual atoms pairing up as dance couples (Lanes, 38).

That senior year, in an interview for the school newspaper, Sendak articulated his beliefs about art that, for the most part, seem to have stayed with him all his life. He said, "Art must advance as rapidly as music; it shouldn't remain static. Artists must try to get away from realism. . . . Instead, we should drift toward expressionism, where personal feelings and pure emotion are put to work" (Lanes, 25). Here Sendak seems to prophesy the basis for some of the best work in his future: the rhythmic illustrations for Ruth Krauss, the colorful expressionism for Charlotte Zolotow's *Mr. Rabbit and the Lovely Present* (1962),[12] and the motivating anger for the beginning of his own *Where the Wild Things Are* (1963).[13]

Because of his aversion to school, Sendak, after graduating from Lafayette in 1946, did not immediately attend art school. He worked instead for a couple of years in a Manhattan window-display company's warehouse. Then in 1948, while working days as a display artist, Sendak took his only formal artistic training at night from the Art Student League in New York (Lanes, 34). He took classes in life drawing and oil painting, but he feels he received the most significant help from his instructor in composition, the illustrator John Groth. Despising an obligatory approach to learning, Sendak responded to Groth's relaxed pedagogy. "[Groth] came in once every two weeks, made some acute criticisms of one's work, and then left one alone," recalls Sendak.[14] Groth's comments on Sendak's work inspired the younger artist to strive for an animated line. As Sendak explains, "[Groth] gave me a sense of the enormous potential for motion, for aliveness, in illustrations" (Lanes, 35). In his own work for adult editions,

Groth illustrated in black-and-white with, as Sendak describes it, "a busy line derived from Daumier" (Lanes, 35). Groth's instruction may have inspired Sendak's early approach to illustrating the junior novels *Maggie Rose: Her Birthday Christmas* (1952),[15] by Ruth Sawyer, and *Shadrach* (1953)[16] and *Hurry Home, Candy* (1953),[17] by Meindert DeJong.

Despite Groth's solid instruction, Sendak did not stay long at the Art Student League: he went for two years and then quit.[18] Looking back, Sendak views this end to his early formal training as detrimental to his art. He confesses, "I am convinced that the surface quality of my work matured slowly because of this inner recoil from formal training. It was not a proud choice; rather, that is how I was temperamentally and psychically—forever tuned out of school" (*Blechman,* 7).

Blossoming with self-reliance, Sendak and his brother, Jack, masterminded a business venture in the summer of 1948. They designed and built elaborate wooden mechanical toys and took them to sell at the posh toy store on Fifth Avenue, F. A. O. Schwarz (FAO). Needless to say, these movable toys were too expensive even for FAO to reproduce in quantity; however, impressed with Maurice's sense of design, the window-display director offered him an assistantship in that department. Sendak accepted and worked there for the next three years (Lanes, 34).

Though his first toys were not moneymaking for FAO, his later toys certainly have been. In 1988 the toy store, commemorating its "fortieth year of friendship" with Sendak, sold limited editions of his stuffed wild thing "Bernard Wild Thing Plush," each personally autographed by Sendak, for $100 each. The anniversary special also featured the video of the opera *Where the Wild Things Are* and the twenty-fifth anniversary edition of the book. FAO arranged its reunion with Sendak to sponsor the premiere of his first edition of *Dear Mili* as well. In its "Ultimate Toy Catalogue" FAO gives Sendak top billing, headlining the flier "Maurice Sendak & FAO."[19]

FAO can boast of its befriending Sendak because the store served as Sendak's own yellow brick road to the land of children's books. At FAO, Sendak first encountered the artwork of the nineteenth-century illustrators he claimed for his lifelong mentors: George Cruikshank, Walter Crane, and Randolph Caldecott. The toy store's book department filled its shelves with holdings by these and other greats, both classical and contemporary. Sendak's frequent presence in this department led him to become acquainted with FAO's buyer for children's books at the time. When she learned that Sendak hoped himself to illustrate children's books, she introduced him to a person who would become highly influential in his career's success, the impresario of children's books at Harper and Brothers, Ursula Nordstrom (Lanes, 35). In meeting Nordstrom, his soon-to-be editor, Sendak stood at the threshold of realizing his hope to become a gainfully employed artist.

Though not at all interested in school, Sendak was interested in teachers. He was starving for good ones, and Nordstrom became one of his best. At age 22, Sendak beat a well-worn path to her office. "Those beginning years revolved around my trips to the old Harper offices on Thirty-third Street and being fed books by Ursula, as well as encouraged with every drawing I did," says Sendak (Lanes, 38).

As Sendak's editor and mentor, Nordstrom made it possible for him to support himself through illustrating. She arranged his first illustrating job for a children's book, Marcel Ayme's The Wonderful Farm (1951)[20] (Lanes, 38). Then in 1952, when Nicolas Mordinoff, an established illustrator, turned down her offer, Nordstrom asked Sendak to illustrate A Hole Is to Dig[21] for Ruth Krauss. Hole created a critical sensation and enjoyed high sales, a success that led to a financially solvent Sendak at age 24. He left his job with FAO and moved out of his parents' house and into his own apartment in Greenwich Village.

Stubbornly chiseling out his own education by finding his own teachers, Sendak began to pursue his lifelong study of learning from other artists and writers. Krauss became Sendak's next great instructor. "Ruth was an experienced children's-book author and a wonderfully patient teacher," says Sendak. "She was my school" (Lanes, 42). Krauss personally tutored Sendak in innovative formats for children's books. Besides traveling up and down Thirty-third Street to Ursula Nordstrom's office, Sendak spent much time at the Eighth Street Bookshop, which he describes as the center of his universe in 1952 (*Blechman,* 7). That bookshop was heaven for Sendak in the fifties because he could linger over books there as long as he liked "without surly gibes from the salesclerks" (*Blechman,* 7).

There Sendak discovered the cartoonist R. O. Blechman's volume *The Juggler of Our Lady* (1952). Sendak was taken with the sheer artistry of the book's design. The slender book was bound in "dusky gray-blue paper" (*Blechman,* 7), and its gold spine caught Sendak's eye because Blechman had hand-lettered the title rather than using a neat typeset. Inside the cover, Blechman had done all the lettering himself, even the copyright and title pages. Blechman told the story in cartoon pictures, using a thin squiggly line. *Juggler* inspired the young Sendak to pursue the making of books, not just the illustrating of them. He explains, "It offered hope that one day I too might have autonomous control of a published work; that every detail, so crucial to the whole, could be rendered by the artist. It also encouraged the latent wish to write one's own book and thus create—through story, pictures, type, layout, binding, choice of paper (and weight of paper), an overall design—a firm, personal statement" (*Blechman,* 8). Sendak realized this dream 10 and 20 years later with the creations of his own picture books.

In 1953 Sendak broadened his self-education with a trip to Europe. In the Louvre he saw paintings by Titian, da Vinci, and Raphael. He was also greatly impressed by the villages of southern France. Back in the United States, he incorporated these impressions into his illustrations for the French author Ayme's *The Magic Pictures* (1954)[22] (Lanes, 51).

Besides being the year he first visited Europe, 1953 marked another milestone in Sendak's private life. At 25 he was showing promise in his career but felt lonely. At that point, he began what would become a 14-year relationship by bringing home a Sealyham terrier whom he named Jennie. As Lanes describes her, Jennie became more to Sendak than a pet: "She was a baby, child, companion, and best friend" (156).

The scruffy terrier makes several guest appearances in Sendak's illustrations. This bearded lady performs quite a number of acts: as Baby in *Kenny's Window,* she pretends she is an elephant (1956);[23] she hangs from a chandelier in Sesyle Joslin's *What Do You Say, Dear?* (1958);[24] and she rides on a sled in *One Was Johnny* (1962).[25] And Jennie is given the limelight in Sendak's own tribute to her, *Higglety Pigglety Pop! or There Must Be More to Life* (1967).[26]

In the first five years of working with Nordstrom, Sendak gained steady work. He collaborated repeatedly with Marcel Ayme, Ruth Krauss, Meindert DeJong, and Beatrice de Regnier. He was, in short, doing well. By age 27, Sendak undertook the illustrating and writing of his own first book, *Kenny's Window* (1956). The task elicited tortuous effort from Sendak, without the desired results. Sendak later viewed the finished book as having "ghastly" illustrations and a "long-winded" narrative (Lanes, 66). Yet for Sendak, *Kenny's Window* was his chance to say all at once everything he wanted to say in a children's book. In it he wove a tangle of his favorite themes—fantasy, fear, and the problems of children.

For the next seven years, Sendak began to unravel these themes by writing and illustrating his own book about every two years. With each publication, Sendak drew nearer his goal of creating a picture book for children. In 1957 he wrote and illustrated *Very Far Away.*[27] The narrative is much leaner than that in *Kenny's Window,* but even in this brief story the conceit becomes redundant as individual wishes are repeated for each character— the horse, the sparrow, the cat, and Martin.

In 1960 Sendak wrote *The Sign on Rosie's Door,*[28] and in 1962 he created four tiny books published under one casing as *The Nutshell Library.*[29] The latter received Sendak's first professional kudos for his solo efforts, garnering an American Library Association [ALA] Notable Book award. The characters in these last five works were so lively and playfully dramatic—the imaginative, flamboyant Rosie and the defiant Pierre—that Sendak proceeded to animate the books for film and stage. Fifteen years later, in 1975, CBS-TV aired Sendak's 30-minute animated film entitled "Maurice Sendak's Really Rosie: Starring the Nutshell Kids," with music by Carole King, as a television special. It was such a success that Sendak and King went on to re-create a musical-play version, *Really Rosie,* first produced off-Broadway in 1980 (Commire, 182).

By age 34, Sendak had illustrated 50 books, writing 7 of those himself, and yet, like his heroine Jennie in *Higglety Pigglety, Pop!* he was seeking "something more." He later described these early books as "too tender for [his] tastes, traditional in the worst ways" (Shirk, 4). He was ready to create a masterpiece—and a controversy.

When Sendak brought out his first picture book, *Where the Wild Things Are,* in 1963, he created both. Most critics agreed the book looked refreshingly imaginative, but many feared the effect it might have on children. Parents and educators worried that the pictures of the wild things, with their sharp teeth and claws, might frighten youngsters. In the *Journal of Nursery Education*'s review, one critic wrote, "We should not like to have it left about where a sensitive child might find it to pore over in the twilight."[30] As Sendak recalls, some critics considered the book "ugly" and "far-fetched" (Shirk, 4). Probably the most damaging criticism for *Wild Things* came from a man who, at the time, had not yet read the book: the child psychologist Bruno Bettelheim.

Ladies' Home Journal carried a monthly column featuring Bettelheim in dialogue with mothers on topics of child rearing. In the March 1969 issue one mother voiced her concern over the scary subject matter of Sendak's picture book without naming either the title or the author, though both were obvious. Bettelheim cautioned mothers against the story, even though he had not read *Wild Things* at the time. His counsel worked against the book insidiously by reinforcing his readers' worst fear, that of being a bad parent. He warned mothers that the story expressed desertion on two accounts: when Max is sent alone to bed and when his mother withholds supper from him. According to Bettelheim, these two actions might evoke anxiety in a child.[31] He argued that "what [Sendak] failed to understand is the incredible fear it evokes in the child to be sent to bed without supper, and this by the first and foremost giver of food and security—his mother" (Bettelheim 1969, 48). Bettelheim charged Sendak with misrepresenting how to deal with "destructive fantasies" (48). Although the following year Mary-Agnes Taylor published a brilliant rebuttal of Bettelheim in the *Horn Book Magazine*,[32] a journal for elementary educators and librarians, *Ladies' Home Journal* had a wider circulation. The damage had been done before the larger audience. Consequently, the picture book was not popular with the general public at first. Most of its support came from the guardians of Caldecott Medal winners: librarians. Sendak explains that *Wild Things* "really started out as a library book, because librarians liked it, and only became successful over time" (Shirk, 4).

And what a success it became. The year following its creation, Sendak was awarded the 1964 Caldecott Medal for the best picture book of the year. From this point, *Wild Things* gradually acquired the status of a classic. By the end of 1987, *Wild Things,* approaching its twenty-fifth anniversary, had "sold nearly two million copies in English," been translated into 16 languages, and been transposed into an opera with the British composer Oliver Knussen supplying the music.[33] And Sendak, a bachelor all his life, has adopted Max, the protagonist of *Wild Things,* as his own child: "How many people have a child who goes out and does so well by them?" he says. "Max is the kind of son I should have been for my parents" (Holland, 44).

In 1967–68, the prospering Sendak experienced one of the worst years of his life. He lost his mother; his dog, Jennie; and nearly his own life. At the time, Sendak had gone to England, where, during a television interview, he suddenly took ill. Unable to continue speaking, he halted the interview and returned to his lodgings. Soon after, Sendak, under the care of a physician, learned he had suffered a serious heart attack (Lanes, 151); he was not quite 39 at the time (*C&C,* 196). Sendak felt shocked at the nearness of dying. "I was amazed," he says. "I couldn't believe it was happening—that my mission could be cut short like that" (Lanes, 151).

While Sendak was recovering in a British nursing home, a friend wired him from America that Jennie had become gravely ill (Harris, 825). Against his physicians' orders, Sendak flew home to New York. He moved himself and Jennie to Fire Island to convalesce together. Though Sendak recuperated, Jennie did not. He had to ask a friend to have the dog put to sleep (Lanes, 153).

During this time, Sendak's mother had cancer. Sendak opted not to tell his parents of his heart attack, so as to spare them worry; he arranged for a friend to send postcards from him from various points in Europe as if he were still traveling (Lanes, 152). When Sendak returned to New York he learned that Sadie's condition had worsened. She died a year later (Lanes, 153).

Ironically, these three events inspired what has been described as "one of [Sendak's] most joyous picture books"—*In the Night Kitchen* (Commire, 27: 192). As a cathartic effort, Sendak had written *Higglety Pigglety Pop!* to work through his grief for Jennie; it came out barely a month after her death (Lanes, 154). Working through his mother's death was more difficult for Sendak (Lanes, 154): it took him two years to create an expression of gratitude for her and for his own survival. *Night Kitchen*, in part, pays homage to her and to Sendak's childhood years with her. As Sendak says, "I wanted to do a book that would say goodbye to New York and say goodbye to my parents, and tell a little bit about the narrow squeak I had just been through" (Shirk, 4). Though Sendak dedicates *Night Kitchen* to his parents, he almost dedicates the plot to himself. "The fact that [Mickey] nearly croaked while he was being baked alive was symbolic of my narrow squeak," he explains (Shirk, 4).

The controversy that surrounded *Wild Things,* which concerned the book's appropriateness for children, was to greet *Night Kitchen* as well. The blatant sensuousness and suggestive sensuality of the book drew scathing reviews from educators. Two impassioned reviews appeared in *Elementary English,* the first of which found Sendak's illustrations brazen for a child in primary school: "It just may be that America's children have been waiting with bated breath for this opportunity to vicariously wallow nude in cake dough and skinny dip in milk—not to mention the thrill of kneading, punching, pounding and pulling. Somehow, I doubt it."[34] The critic concludes that Sendak has "struck a literary blow for the Kid Lib movement" (Root, 263). The second review condemned the narrative of *Night Kitchen* for what the critic felt to be its confusing suggestiveness, describing the picture book as "questionable nourishment for the very young members of our society."[35] Librarians and educators seemed most troubled by Mickey's frontal nudity. As Sendak said, this aspect at first caused the book to be banned: "Unbeknownst to me, there had never been a picture of a frontal nude child in an American children's book. The only way it could be seen in many schools was if the teacher drew clothes on the child. The controversy reduced the book to such a stupid level" (Shirk, 4). Sendak favors *Night Kitchen* over *Wild Things,* yet it never became as popular with the public (Lanes, 189).

Though some American critics balked at Sendak's audacity in 1970, several international ones applauded. They crowned Sendak as the first American illustrator to receive the Hans Christian Andersen Award, an honor paralleling the Nobel Prize in children's literature (Lanes, 26, 7). In his acceptance speech, Sendak articulated the turning point he saw in his career's direction. Specifically, he wanted to create picture books. Sendak clarified his renewed vision by saying, "I no longer want simply to illustrate—or, for that matter, simply to write. I am now in search of a form more purely and essentially my own. In a way I'd rather have been a composer of operas and songs . . . where music and words mix and blend and incredibly excite, defines my ideal" ("Andersen," 7). Here Sendak also foreshadows a later turning point in his art toward opera.

Sendak has never been one to rest on his laurels; if anything, the more praise he receives, the harder he seems to work. The year he received the Andersen Award, he undertook meticulous preparations to illustrate a collection of Grimm tales newly translated by Lore Segel. The collection would be titled *The Juniper Tree and Other Tales from Grimm,* published in two volumes by

Michael di Capua at Farrar, Straus, and Giroux in 1973 (Lanes, 191–92).[36] Sendak's work on *Juniper Tree* marks his first interpretive illustrating of the tales of the Grimm brothers, Wilhelm and Jacob. He expressed his preference for the vintage Grimms' fairy tales much earlier, in a 1964 essay, when he noted that they offered "a real world distilled into fantasy" (*C&C,* 159).

To engender an authentic flavor in his illustrations, Sendak set sail for Germany in 1971, seeking to study the actual landscape and culture that cultivated the Grimms' stories. He viewed the Grimm Museum in Kassel, a "Sleeping Beauty castle" in Karlshafen, a stunning forest in Reinhardswold, the medieval architecture of Goslar, plus many original etchings by Dürer (1471–1528) (Lanes, 195). Sendak hoped this pilgrimage would prevent his illustrations from portráying "just an American, 1970s point of view" (Lanes, 193).

In the end, Sendak illustrated *Juniper Tree* much as a composer writes a pasticcio, by borrowing fragments and motifs from various sources of his trip and memory. He quotes from the medieval, renaissance, and romantic periods, producing an eclectic style, one praised by Paul Heins in his review of the book.[37] In critiquing Sendak's picture for the tale "The Two Journeymen," Heins writes, "There is the powerful suggestion of a painted Crucifixion as it might have been delineated by a Flemish painter or depicted by Salvador Dali" (Heins, 138). For Heins, the strength of Sendak's wide-ranging quotations is that Sendak selects the image most responsive to the particular story (138).

The same year Sendak brought out *Juniper Tree* he published another lighthearted version of the Grimms' tale *King Grisly-Beard: A Tale from the Brothers Grimm* (1973).[38] Unlike the brooding, black-and-white drawings for *Juniper Tree,* Sendak's illustrations for *Grisly-Beard* flaunt the color, layout, and bubble language of a comic strip. Sendak improvises on Edgar Taylor's 1823 translation not by altering the text in any way but by adding his own narrative through cartoonlike boxes at the bottom of the pages. In his cartoon drawings, Sendak stages the tale as an operatic production. Before Taylor's text begins, Sendak draws on the book's initial endpaper a runty boy and girl reading a sign that says THEATER STRAIGHT AHEAD. On the following title page, Sendak draws himself dressed in the nineteenth-century hat and tails of an impresario. He is posting an advertisement that notes,

> WANTED!
> Extraordinary
> Actor & Actress
> To Play The
> Leading Roles
> In Wilhelm &
> Jacob Grimm's
> Fabulous
> King Grisly-Beard
> Inquire Within   (*Grisly-Beard,* n.p.)

On the dedication page, Sendak pictures the boy and girl donning their costumes and crowns for the show. By the time Taylor has said "Once upon a time," the boy and girl are in character, voicing their one-word lines in comic-strip bubbles. Sendak's trick is clever, cute, and a little corny; however, projecting himself into the role of an impresario was soon to be more than a joke.

In the late seventies Frank Corsaro offered Sendak his dream, asking Sendak to assist him in staging operas. At the time, Sendak replied, "It's been a dream of mine all my life, but I'm mired in children's books. Who would take a chance on such a person?"[39] Obviously, Corsaro would and did. To date, he and Sendak have collaborated on six operas. The compatible duo seem literally and figuratively to see eye to eye on how to stage opera, both of them being under six feet (Corsaro, 11).

Throughout the 1980s, Corsaro and Sendak produced their operas across America and throughout Europe. Their productions became known for their spectacular staging effects. In 1979 the Houston Grand Opera commissioned Corsaro to direct and Sendak to design the costumes and sets for Mozart's *Magic Flute.* For this show, Sendak created a "smoke-belching dragon and a hot-air balloon that brings the three angelic singers onto the stage."[40]

This version of *Flute* was revived by the Opera and Music Theatre Institute of Newark, New Jersey, in 1988–89 (Clemons, 52). In yet another spectacular performance of Mozart, Sendak and Corsaro's version of *Idomeneo* premiered in 1990 at the Los Angeles Music Center.[41]

Also in 1979, UNESCO commissioned the two to produce an opera of *Wild Things* to commemorate the International Year of the Child (Cech, 306). This show opened in Brussels in 1980, with its music scored by Knussen. In 1984 the Glyndebourne Opera at London's National Theatre resurrected the show with fuller effects added by Sendak. Here Sendak had Max's mother run a "huge 1930s vacuum cleaner" across the stage (Cech, 307). In addition, five gargantuan wild things loomed from 9 to 12 feet in height, demanding three persons each to operate. As a special effect, one of the wild things "[lost] its head during the wild rumpus scene—which [was] done as a kind of Stravinskian 'Rite of Spring'" (Cech, 308). This version of *Wild Things* premiered in the United States with the Minnesota Opera in 1985.

Prokofiev's *Love for Three Oranges* proved to be one of the collaborators' most challenging shows. It ran successfully at the Glyndebourne Opera in England in 1982 and was revived by the New York City Opera in 1985 (Clemons, 52). Initially, however, Corsaro and Sendak saw little promise in the opera. "The libretto was devoid of the kind of human conflict Maurice and I doted on," explains Corsaro (11). Hence, the two artists deliberately spiced up Prokofiev's scheme. To intensify the venom of Princess Clarice, Sendak suggested she fire guns at her servants. "That would make her truly rotten," quipped Sendak. "After all, that's what servants were there for in the eighteenth century" (Corsaro, 63). Most memorable is Corsaro and Sendak's rendition of Fata Morgana, the witch in *Love,* whose image Sendak reproduced onto a huge, inflatable balloon (Cech, 310). Much as he did for his wild things, Sendak drew inspiration for Fata from his intruding Sunday relatives, bearing in mind "the perfect model" (Corsaro, 66). Further into the opera, Sendak delighted the audience by rigging "a nightmarish pop-up version of the *In the Night Kitchen* . . .

chefs" (Cech, 310). As John Cech describes the event, the British audience, "in their black ties and tiaras, abandoned all restraint and screamed with delight, like a group of children" (311).

In 1981 Corsaro and Sendak produced Janacek's *Cunning Little Vixen* in New York. Taken from the Czech writer Rudolf Tesnohlidek's novel by the same (English-edition) name, *Vixen* offered Sendak one of his favorite tropes for the drama of the human soul: Tesnohlidek satirizes the predicaments of human beings through wild things; specifically, Tesnohlidek wittily records the picaresque adventures of vixen Sharp-Ears as if she were a woman out on her own in the world. Robert Jones, one of the translators for Sendak's illustrated-book version of the novel, describes the way Tesnohlidek's conceit works: "It presents a world of not-so-innocent animals living out their short lives in brutal harmony alongside a world of longer-lived humans who are no less brutal, scarcely more intelligent, and a good deal less happy."[42] Sendak cleverly exploits this conceit through his costumes, dressing up human characters as animals and animal characters as human beings (Cech, 310). In what seemed to be an irremediable tragedy, Sendak's costumes, while in storage, were destroyed by a fire in 1985. Nevertheless, the New York City Opera chose Corsaro and Sendak's version of *Vixen* for its production in 1989 (Clemons, 52). Sendak's costumes can be viewed at anytime, of course, as illustrations in the book *Vixen*. It is pure conjecture, but the ending illustration of "Golden-Stripe, the yellow-furred fox from the Deep Ravine" expresses a likeness of Sendak's temperament that may well be a playful self-portrait. In his own golden years, Sendak could just have easily been portrayed, as Sharp-Ears describes Golden-Stripe, as "no novice in this world, no young dandy just pushed out of mama's den" (Tesnohlidek, 137).

In 1985 Corsaro and Sendak teamed up with Knussen again to produce an opera of *Higglety Pigglety Pop!* at the request of the BBC. Their production appeared at the Glyndebourne Festival as a lyrical companion piece to the boisterous *Wild Things*. Because *Higglety Pigglety Pop!* works from a quieter, comic mood, Sendak restrained the big-top circus acts. Instead, he created much fun by dressing up the singers as the book's characters—a terrier, a lion, and a baby "who nearly steals the show" (Cech, 313).

Besides designing stage sets for operas during the 1980s, Sendak also collaborated with Kent Stowell, the artistic director of the Pacific Northwest Ballet, on a production of *Nutcracker*.[43] Sendak was at first reluctant to accept the commission for a ballet until he realized Stowell shared his own innovative vision for unpredictability, psychological tension, and faithfulness to a work's artistic roots. With such mutual agreement, the two men resurrected E. T. A. Hoffman's original subplot entitled "The Story of the Hard Nut" for their opera (*Nutcracker*, xi–xii). Their unprecedented version of *Nutcracker* premiered in Seattle in 1983 (*Nutcracker*, xiv). As with the memorabilia for *Vixen*, Sendak followed up his ballet adventure with an illustrated-book version entitled *Nutcracker* (1984).

Then in his fifties, Sendak seemed rejuvenated by his plunge into stage designing. The art of the operatic spectacle began immediately to influence his original medium of illustration. He confided in a letter to Corsaro, "I think you will agree that the rather stripped compositions in *The Juniper Tree* and even the seemingly cluttered but rather intense and concentrated composition in *Outside Over There* already suggest a growing awareness of—what?—stage sense? Certainly working with you on *Flute* and *Vixen* has developed this new sense of theatrical composition" (Corsaro, 88). The lavishness of operatic theater sets the stage in *Outside Over There* with Sendak's draped folds in the flowing gowns of Ida and her mother and with his mist hovering like dry ice in the background.

Selma Lanes records in her biography that the art in *Outside Over There* also alludes to many personal meanings for the artist beyond the public domain. Sendak pays tribute to the silver-screen memories of his childhood by dressing Ida in the blue dress of Judy Garland from *The Wizard of Oz*. He models the kidnapping in his story after his childhood fear of the kidnapping of Charles Lindbergh, Jr., with the exception that his baby is saved (Shirk, 4). His plot line also pivots on Ida's having to look after her baby sister as Natalie had to look after Maurice (Lanes, 235).

Even Ida's name stems from Sendak's past, echoing that of a favorite woman in his old neighborhood (Lanes, 234).

The critical reception to *Outside Over There* was as mixed as its sources. Though the picture book won a silver honor medal from the Caldecott committee, some critics who had praised Sendak's earlier work were disappointed with this later one. Donnarae MacCann and Olga Richard found the book's private symbolism of Sendak difficult for children to interpret. In addition, they believed that the structure of *Outside Over There* did not have the unity of *Wild Things*.[44]

At this point in his career, Sendak could afford for some critics not to like his work; his ever-burgeoning royalties seemed boundless in the 1980s, stemming in part from the upward trend in children's publishing. Sendak referred to the remarkable increase in sales of children's books during the 1980s as a type of "spontaneous combustion," so fast and furious did the boom in the business occur.[45] From 1978 to 1988 alone Harper and Row's storied children's division witnessed an increase in profit from $14 million to $40 million (Nocera, 54).

The market for Sendak's books continued to be so great that when he came out with *Dear Mili* in 1988, it made "publishing history" (Rothstein, 13). Its first printing ran at the "unheard of figure" of 250,000 copies, with 230,000 of those already spoken for at printing time; until Sendak's success, the largest first printings for other children's books ran from 100,000 to 140,000 copies (Rothstein, 13).

Mili also made history, or, more aptly, "remade it," because Sendak was illustrating a previously unpublished story by Wilhelm Grimm that had been discovered only during the mid-1980s.[46] Grimm had included the story in an 1816 letter to a girl named "Mili." Sendak was drawn to the tale's account of a young child who perseveres during her separation from her mother in wartime; however, at the end of the story, when she is reunited with her mother, Grimm has the two die after one cheerful evening together. At the time of the book's debut, Sendak anticipated some critics' objections to his working with disturbing themes again, this time those of war, separation, and death (Rothstein, 13).

Ironically, just the opposite happened in one review. Janet Adam Smith was disappointed with what she saw as Sendak's euphemistic handling of these themes in his illustrations; she criticized those illustrations for being too charming, intimating that Sendak had compromised his artistic vision.[47] Basing her judgment heavily on Sendak's earlier illustrations of the Grimm tales collected in *Juniper Tree,* Smith felt *Mili* paled by comparison. "It is a pretty book that will please many," she wrote, "but it has nothing of the impact of *The Juniper Tree*" (Smith, 26). Moreover, she poked fun at Sendak's censoring of the angel's anatomy this time, in contrast to Mickey's exposure in *Night Kitchen* (26).

At the time he finished the pictures for *Mili,* Sendak was 60 and exhibiting all the signs of quickening rather than slowing his creative pace. In 1988 he was rushing to complete three projects at the same time: illustrations for *Mili,* the production and designs for the opera *Idomeneo,* and a collection of his essays and speeches entitled *Caldecott & Co.: Notes on Books & Pictures* (Rothstein, 13). *Caldecott & Co.* is full of numerous addresses and essays from various occasions, attesting to the hectic schedule Sendak has kept up as a public speaker. As Olive Ann Burns—herself the author at 60 of the hit novel *Cold Sassy Tree*—once said, "Writers write, authors speak."[48] At age 62, Sendak opened and closed his year with speaking engagements. He started 1989 with the opening-night speech for the Village-Writers-Meet-Their-Neighbors series in New York;[49] he closed the year with an address to more than 900 Washington University students in St. Louis (Shirk, 1). At the end of that particular lecture, "scores of college students, among the first generation to grow up on his stories, offered up tattered copies of his books for autographs" (Shirk, 1). Just as its author, *Wild Things* had come of age without becoming outdated.

In the celebration of Passover, during the Order of the Seder the Jewish family sings, "Of three matzos on the tray, take one piece to hide away." Similar to that young child who tucks the matzo away for later, Sendak saved his desire for designing operas until later; then his matzo multiplied plenteously. Sendak's aptitude for working with art forms as disparate as the picture

2

Early Illustration: Duets with Krauss, Minarik, and DeJong

From the beginning of his career as an illustrator, Maurice Sendak drew inspiration for the way his art should work from the way music works. He sought to re-create the energy of music in his static medium of pictures. To do this, his task was twofold: to capture the creative spirit of the author's text and to animate that idea technically.[1]

During this early period, Sendak formed three chief allegiances with the writers Ruth Krauss, Else Holmelund Minarik, and Meindert DeJong. His style of illustration differed completely for each author, bearing witness to his already-firm conviction that his illustrations should empathize specifically with each narrative. As a young illustrator in his twenties, Sendak faced technical problems of transferring his desire for animation into lines and color. Krauss, Minarik, and DeJong served as steady mentors, modeling in their words a vitality with which Sendak could collaborate in his pictures. To collaborate, Sendak did not merely duplicate the images each author gave in her or his text. By analogy, he did not sing in unison with these writers; rather, he learned to sing in duet, singing in the same key or tone, yet embellishing their score or text with his own supporting improvisation. Early on, then, Sendak's pictures work together with the author's words to present the whole song, or world, of the book.

Collaboration with Krauss

A Hole Is to Dig

"The musical analogy and its relevance to my own work is nowhere more apparent than in my illustrations for the picturebooks of Ruth Krauss," wrote Sendak in 1964 ("Shape of Music," 205). Indeed, Sendak's collaboration with Krauss inspired an energy and a punctuated rhythm for his art that have had lasting effects on his entire career. As if singing a duet with her, Sendak learned to listen sensitively to the melody, tempo, and tone of Krauss's lyrics to gauge his own illustrative harmony.

In Krauss and Sendak's first book together, *A Hole Is to Dig: A First Book of First Definitions* (1952), the words and pictures together create a mood of spontaneity. As its title suggests, *Hole* is not a story; it is a collection of the endearingly odd understandings children use to explain ordinary words. Before Sendak joined her, Ruth Krauss acquired a child's perspective for the book by gleaning the actual words of youngsters. She visited preschools to hear and record the live speech of pupils (Lanes, 42). By listening to these children, Krauss gathered many unusual definitions for words: "Dogs are to kiss people," "Hands are to hold," and "The world is so you have something to stand on" (*Hole,* n.p.). She then arranged these sayings so as to be as lively and fresh as the day they were said.

Krauss's arrangement of the children's language creates a sense of spontaneity because it combines repetition with variation. Her method is strikingly similar to that of composing a musical theme with variations. Krauss announces her theme to the reader both directly and indirectly through the title—*A Hole Is to Dig: A First Book of First Definitions*—and thereby alerts the reader to listen for her recurring motif of a definition in the "x is to y" format, in particular, for the definition of a "hole." Using seven different explanations for "hole," Krauss creates an expected rhythm in the text by repeating a definition for "hole" about every three pages, beginning with "A hole is to dig" and then adding a few pages later "A hole is to sit in" and a few pages farther "A hole is to plant a flower." Likewise, she repeats definitions for "hands," "noses," and "toes." Yet to keep the phrasing from sounding too predictable, she periodically alters the phrasing.

For surprises throughout the text, Krauss tucks into the corners of pages asides that are not definitions. After the regular definition at the top of the page, in large letters, of "The sun is to tell you when it's everyday," Krauss whispers her aside in small letters in the corner: "When you make your bed you get a star." While the reader expects the repetition of the definitions, she or he does not expect the unprecedented asides—"Oo! A rock is when you trip on it you should have watched where you were going."

Sendak's illustrations complement Krauss's rhythmic pattern of repetition with variation. Sendak decorates the book's endpapers with a design that serves as something of an overture to the book illustrations' reflection of this theme. At first glance, the design seems random: it sports four different children dancing in five rows, each dancer leaping and kicking in a different way, the order of the four dancers seemingly altered in each row. On closer examination, it is apparent that Sendak has created the feeling of frolic and fun through calculated repetition: he has repeated the order of the dancers in the first and last rows, suggesting a sense of completeness; he has presented two dancers facing the viewer and two facing away, creating a checkered effect; and he has placed an even number of figures in an odd number of rows, lining up the same figures diagonally.

In the book's illustrations Sendak continues to both repeat and vary designs in his layout patterns, alternating moods. He uses four major layout patterns, evoking different degrees of energy. Whereas the double spreads of large groups suggest rambunctious activity, the single pages of small groups connote lively, less boisterous play. And the single pages of a solitary figure, as well as the corners of pages holding one or two characters, portray quiet moods. By alternating pictures of solitary figures with pictures of groups, and single pages depicting small groups with the double spreads, Sendak creates regular mood swings from busy to serene.

This sense of rhythmic visual pacing came during revision of the book. Sendak relied heavily on Krauss for advice on how to arrange his pictures with her words (Lanes, 42). In his original sketches Sendak filled in the backgrounds with scenery and land-scapes.[2] Later Krauss and Sendak isolated many of the figures and props, leaving the background empty, except in the busy dou-ble spreads.

The layout designs of Sendak's illustrations also parallel simi-lar subjects in Krauss's text. For the parallel definitions of "Dogs are to kiss people" and "Cats are so you can have kittens," Sendak provides parallel layout patterns: two double spreads, one with so many dogs that each child has her or his own, and the other with so many kittens that each child has at least two for company. For the parallel definitions of what certain body parts are for— "Toes are to dance on" and "Hands are to hold"—Sendak employs parallel layout designs of small groups dancing on each page with isolated figures in the corners.

The vitality and capriciousness of *Hole* come from a highly dis-ciplined approach to the collaboration of words and pictures. Just as Sendak's layout patterns reinforce Krauss's parallel subjects, so too do Krauss's asides accompany Sendak's solitary figures in the corners of pages, never appearing as the main text headlined at the top. And most important, Krauss and Sendak keep the words and pictures uncluttered. With few exceptions, Krauss lim-its her definitions to one per page. Sendak limits his details in the drawings, letting cross-hatching provide a sense of depth and change in the values. This simplicity lets the spontaneity of the book shine.

A Very Special House

In these collaborators' next work, *A Very Special House* (1953), Krauss's words and Sendak's pictures express the same idea in the same tone. This book does not tell a story but, rather, enacts the imaginary play of a little boy. The main idea of *Special House* is that the little boy is pretending; consequently, the book's tone is as playful as its subject. From beginning to end, the little boy amuses himself by imagining a house complete with an entourage of his own make-believe playmates.

What is significant about Krauss's writing style is that she is able to re-create the little boy's imaginary world without directly saying it is imaginary until the end. She establishes that the boy's special house is make-believe in three ways. First, she introduces the fictive setting by using nonsense words. In the first line of text, the boy sings to himself, "dee dee dee oh-h-h."[3] Second, she makes the unfolding lyrics illogical. The boy continues to sing that the chairs are not for sitting in and the table is not for eating on. Third, Krauss veritably re-creates the world of his imagination by introducing the absurd residents of his house: a giant, a dead mouse, monkeys, "skunkeys," and a lion. It is not until the penultimate page of narrative that Krauss lets the boy explain directly that this very special house is located "root in the moodle of [his] head head head."

Sendak's pictures work appropriately with Krauss's text because they also delineate, through their color and line, what is make-believe from what is not. Sendak signals that the boy is real by depicting only him in color: in blue overalls, with white for his shirt and skin, the boy stands out, almost as a cutout, from the remaining golden background. Likewise, Sendak signals that the rest of the playmates are imaginary by limiting them to line drawings without color. Moreover, he adopts a child's style of drawing for the imaginary characters. He draws a looped line for the donkey's mane and sticks for legs on the squirrels and monkeys. Driving the point home, Sendak pictures, on the third page of text, the boy himself, crayon in hand, drawing lollipop trees and stick-legged animals to show that the boy is creating these fantastic images himself.

Sendak's choice to imitate the style of children's drawings appears to have been as avant-garde at the time as Krauss's choice to use the actual words of children. In a 1958 survey of contemporary artists Sendak is commended as one taking the "new approach"—an approach that involves, explains the critic, drawing "pictures not that children will like, but that will be close to those that a child himself might do."[4] The critic concedes that Sendak's success stems from the way his graphic style complements Krauss's verbal one—in short, that since the books' audience is very young children, "the prime necessity is for simple statements [to be] simply presented" (Ward, 33). Unfortunately, the critic seems more concerned with what is best for children than with how Sendak's art delights them.

Krauss's text and Sendak's illustrations engage their audience because they exude the same playful tone. They do so in two ways. First, Sendak's layout designs complement the rhythmic energy of Krauss's text, which emphatically repeats words for strong beats in the lines. In the following passage she repeats the phrase "very special" at the end of lines, and she repeats the word "feet" at the end of the entire stanza:

There's a bed that's very special
and a shelf that's very special
and the chairs are very special
—but it's not to take a seat—
and the doors are very special
and the walls are very special and
a table very special where to put your feet feet feet.

In accord with the verbal energy of Krauss, Sendak, on this same page, uses the repetition of a visual image to animate the accompanying picture. He draws the boy four times, making a circle round the block of text. In each picture the boy assumes a different action—drawing, climbing, sleeping, and sitting. As Joseph Schwarcz notes in *Ways of the Illustrator,* "This repetition of the figure indicates motion from one point to another and also the passing of time."[5] Because the boy's image circles the text, the layout design further suggests a cycle, possibly the recurring habit of the boy's daydreaming.

Second, Krauss's words and Sendak's pictures also capture the same whimsical tone because as she plays with the language, Sendak plays with the graphics. Krauss creates a type of nursery bebop using coined words and improvising on a theme; she uses a children's "scat" vocabulary of "hooie," "ooie," "ret in the meedle," and "blop blop blop," making the tone of the text comical. Sendak makes the illustrations ostensibly comical by employing the cartoon technique of showing visible sound (Schwarcz, 77): when the lion eats the stuffing, he hums, "M-M-M-M"; when the skunk whispers to the boy, he utters, "Psss—ss"; and when the boy falls on his bottom, written by his knee in capital letters is the visible sound word "BUNG." These verbal codes mimic the stereotyped onomatopoeic spellings from comic books and readily clue the reader in to the realm of humor and fun. In addition, Krauss parallels her comical words with comical actions. For instance, she improvises on the lion's role to be "eating all the stuffings from the chairs chairs chairs." In like spirit, Sendak counters her playfulness by illustrating the ridiculous action with a visual pun: when the lion eats the "stuffing," Sendak pictures him becoming stuffed himself, growing from skinny to plump.

When Krauss plays with the text to make it resemble music, Sendak creates that same analogy in his pictures. As in a musical composition, Krauss repeats at the end the same stanza from the beginning, as if it were a refrain:

> I know a house—
> it's not a squirrel house
> it's not a donkey house

When this refrain appears at the end of the book, Sendak mimics the idea of a musical da capo by also repeating his initial illustrations in a type of visual refrain. As the narrative text tapers to a close, he does not crowd the page with images but instead chooses to picture the donkey and squirrels as he did in the beginning. Then, on the next page, echoing his opening illustration, he removes the scenery entirely and pictures the boy alone.

I'll Be You and You Be Me

The year following *Special House,* Krauss and Sendak published *I'll Be You and You Be Me* (1954). In the same avant-garde spirit of their first two collaborations, *I'll Be You* did not tell one story but, rather, offered a mottled collection of brief poems, plays, and anecdotes revolving around the themes of love and friendship. More so than with their first two books, Krauss afforded Sendak the opportunity to elaborate on the meaning of her text. As Sendak would write later in his 1964 essay "The Shape of Music," the "lovely and original poetry [of Krauss] has a flexibility that allowed me the maximum space to execute my fantasy variations on a Kraussian theme" (205). Much of the flexibility in *I'll Be You* stems from the fact that Krauss changes her format from page to page. On one page she gives a poem, on the next a story, and on the following a terse drama. Sendak's illustrations complement this experimental format because he arranges them in the layout of an artist's sketchbook, with whole pages divided into series of small scenarios, similar to dummy pages for a comic-strip narrative. Thus the reader, to interpret *I'll Be You,* must refer back and forth between words and pictures.

Sendak's illustrations specify the details Krauss's lines omit. In one poem Krauss uses the concrete nouns "sun," "house," "river," and "hill" with the more abstract nouns "song" and "dream." She writes,

> I love the sun
> I love a house
> I love a river
> and a hill where I watch
> and a song I heard
> and a dream I made.

On that same verso Sendak literally illustrates these images specified by Krauss, drawing a boy standing beneath the sun on a hill overlooking a house and a river; however, on the accompanying recto Sendak interprets both the "song" and the "dream" as his own embellishment. In an animated series of 12 miniature scenes, he draws the boy looking lost in a wood and perhaps listening, for in the next frame the boy discovers a giant bird. Looking back to the poem's line "a song I heard," the reader may infer that the little boy hears the bird singing. Likewise, looking back to the line "a dream I made," the reader may interpret Sendak's next 6 scenes as specifying that dream. In Sendak's sketches the boy climbs on the huge bird's back to soar for 6 scenes through night and day, over forests and above water, until the bird returns him to his mother, who hugs her son as the bird flies away.

Elsewhere, Krauss's poem suggests a daydream and Sendak's illustrations elaborate. On the left-hand page, Krauss writes,

> shoes shoes
> little black shoes
> little black shoes
> with little black bows—
> someday someday
> little black shoes
> with little black bows
> on the toes—

Although the daydream focuses on the shoes, Sendak's illustrations focus on the dreamer. Embellishing on whom the little black shoes are for, he presents his dreamer—a squatty female child hunched on a stool. Then, through a series of 12 miniature drawings, the illustrations show the metamorphosis of the child into a prima ballerina complete with tiara and tutu. She dances, leaping and swaying for 8 scenes in a row, until in the thirteenth drawing she receives a bouquet of flowers and a shower of blossoms from unpictured admirers. Finally, the illustrations show the ballerina evolve back into the original child, staring wide-eyed from her seat. Sendak's illustrations interpolate the dreamer, the dancer, the dance—almost everything except the shoes.

Yet although Sendak takes great liberties in furnishing the details for Krauss's text, he nevertheless submits to the spirit of her song, especially its sense of rhythm. Krauss arranges the lines to have strong beats, with repetitions of "shoes shoes" and "someday someday." Sendak also arranges his illustrations to have punctuated rhythm. Rhythm is created in graphic art by the repetition of a form.[6] Sendak works strong rhythmic beats into his design with the 8 repetitions of the ballerina dancing, yielding a feeling of animated movement. His repetition of the small, wistful girl at the beginning and end of the daydream yields a sense of quiet rhythmic closure.

Still, in *I'll Be You* Sendak takes one liberty with the illustrations that seems incongruous with the context of Krauss's narrative: whereas Krauss's text exhibits the rhythm, references, and slang of American English, not all of Sendak's illustrations seem to take place in America. Krauss's language assumes the lilt and colloquialisms of American conversation with such lines as "I call 'Honey, come here, Honey,' and he comes." Moreover, she seems to set her tableaux against a Yankee-Doodle backdrop with the reference to "George Washington's Birthday." On the other hand, in several of his backgrounds Sendak pictures a European community, not an American one. He nestles hamlets of domed towers and narrowed tall buildings in the landscapes. In a ditty of a love song, Krauss's text voices American slang and idioms:

> love is the same as like
> only you spell them different—
> only more of the same, sort of—
> Love has more stuff in it!

Sendak accompanies this song with illustrations of a bride and groom, thus adding a nice concrete touch; but, he puts Krauss's American, English-speaking couple into a European landscape. Sendak draws an ox—not the customary American horse—pulling the wedding carriage. Above the scene, he studs the sky with hex signs that seem more at home in the old country than in the new. These disparate details may quietly announce the emerging of a more confident Sendak.

Charlotte and the White Horse

In *Charlotte and the White Horse* Krauss and Sendak create a surreal impression. Krauss weaves a loose story line shaped by palpable feelings rather than actions. In the beginning, Charlotte lavishes praise and affection on her pet horse. When her father commands that she sell the animal to help pay for her brother's college tuition, she is crushed, and so her father allows her to keep her pet. The book ends much as it begins, with more descriptions of Charlotte caring for her pony—she rides, feeds, but most of all visits with her white horse.

Besides her focus on the emotional quality of the narrative, Krauss effects a sense of dreaminess for the book by writing in multiple perspectives. She uses the third, second, and first person without clues as to who is speaking when. This blurring of the narrative parallels the disorientation experienced in some dreams, in which the dreamer is not sure where she is and whom she is with. Besides the switches in pronouns, from "I" to "she," the switches in tone, from abstract to concrete, belie changes in the voicing, as heard in the following passage:

> Arise, my Love, my fair one
> my milk white Milky Way—
> Come away, Pure White,
> All White and Strong
> —stronger than Hero the Great Dog
> —sure, but he couldn't wag his tail like Hero—[7]

Here the opening song is from Charlotte's perspective, as if she is singing to her pony. But its romantic, poetic tone does not concur with the casual tone of the lines following. The whole book sounds as if a poet is singing the story, yet a child keeps interrupting her.

Sendak harmonizes the style of his illustrations with the dreaminess of Krauss's narratives by finding inspiration in one of his favorite surrealist painters, Marc Chagall. While muting Chagall's radical cubist compositions, Sendak nevertheless mimics their multiple perspectives. He draws Milky Way's stable from the perspective of the outside and the inside at the same time. He gives it a two-dimensional roof and a one-dimensional interior, without walls for depth. As if quoting the boxy houses in Chagall's *I and the Village* (1911), Sendak borders his village road in *Charlotte and the White Horse* with similar small houses squeezed tightly together.

Chagall's more obvious influence on Sendak lies in the use of a rich palette of colors. *Charlotte and the White Horse* was "Sendak's first book in full colors." As Lanes notes, because Sendak had previously worked with acetate overlays the color for his illustrations had been dictated by the printers' ink stock available at press time. Working in full color, Sendak could choose his own pigments and shades (Lanes, 53). He chose the royal blues, deep russets, and golden ochers found in the dreamscapes of Chagall.

Open House for Butterflies

After three other collaborations, three years in a row—*I Want to Paint My Bathroom Blue* (1956), *The Birthday Party* (1957), and *Somebody Else's Nut Tree and Other Tales for Children* (1958)— Krauss and Sendak came full circle to end where they began, publishing *Open House for Butterflies* (1960), another version of *Hole*. In *Open House* Krauss again eschews a sequential story line and instead gives the reader a collection of childlike sayings concerning sundry topics. Although the text is not based on a series of definitions, as *Hole* is, *Open House* parallels the same book design as *Hole's*: it is physically the same size (6½ × 5½ inches) and its layout follows the same format, using terse lines and tiny illustrations. But in *Open House* Krauss's text and Sendak's illustrations create a quainter atmosphere than in *Hole*—"quaint" in both senses, that is, unusual and old-fashioned.

Here the subjects of Krauss's aphorisms are zanier than in *Hole*. She toys with idioms: "When you run out of cereal can you run into it again?" she asks.[8] More of her sayings are improbable: "You should make a sad face when you meet a crocodile" and "A queen suit is a good thing to have in case you're planning to be a queen when you grow up." In short, while the subjects of *Hole* were those possible to encounter on a day's stroll down the neighborhood sidewalk—a brother, mud, cats and dogs, even a principal—the subjects of *Open House* reside more often than not in the world of the imagination.

Sendak adjusts his illustrations to be appropriate for the quaint world of *Open House,* specifically by re-creating a nostalgic world—a world hoped for rather than experienced. When Krauss writes, "A good thing to know is this road is private for everybody," Sendak conceptualizes that road with a neighborhood of gingerbread houses. He miniaturizes the houses, sticking over-size signs behind their small picket fences, and caricatures the coziness with Victorian trimming, decorative gables, and neat squares of lawn. In *Hole* Sendak's illustrations depicted scenery more naturalistically. There, behind Krauss's definition of "The ground is to make a garden," the illustration shows an encroach-ing wooden wall with indiscriminate city buildings blocking the view of the sky. In *Open House* the city buildings are adorable. They exhibit turn-of-the-century masonry with cornices above the windows and ornamental ribbed rooftops. Sendak makes the city scenes airy by isolating buildings and trees, one per page. In un-natural tidiness, the laundry hangs neatly between buildings, and the doors of the storm cellar are cleanly swept by a spray of blossoms. Even the trash-can lid is on intact. This time, in *Open House,* Sendak's illustrations evoke a sense of a fanciful world.

Collaboration with Minarik

While still collaborating with Krauss, Sendak in 1957 began his collaboration with Else Holmelund Minarik. Over a decade, they were to create six books together: *No Fighting, No Biting!* (1958), in which a niece and nephew are entertained by their young aunt's alligator stories, and the five readers that make up the *Little Bear* series—*Little Bear* (ALA Notable Book; 1957); *Father Bear Comes Home* (ALA Notable Book; 1959); *Little Bear's Friend* (1960); *Little Bear's Visit* (1961); and *A Kiss for Little Bear* (1968). Each book except the last offers a handful of sketches portraying the domestic escapades of Little Bear in his circle of family and friends—Hen, Duck, Cat, Owl, and Emily. The tone of the series is both clever and tender, as most of the plots turn on Minarik's gentle wit.

That Minarik and Sendak were able to combine their narra-tives and illustrations into such an elegant package as the set of five *Little Bear* books is no small feat considering their assign-ment: to write and illustrate *I Can Read* books, "easy readers" for

Harper and Row. Writers of easy readers face certain challenges. One problem that Dr. Seuss, editor in chief of Beginner Books, points out is that these authors must "endure the pains of writing books using only a mere hand full of words."[9] Two further demands are the required simple-sentence structure and the need for repetition.

In *Little Bear*, the first book of the series, Minarik tailors the easy reader to a short attention span, dividing the nearly 50 pages of text into four vignettes. With each scene, she develops the sparkling imagination of Little Bear and the devoted patience of his mother. In the first episode Little Bear repeatedly asks his mother for articles of clothing to wear on a snowy day, until she strips him down to nothing. Afraid his mother has forgotten his birthday, Little Bear, in the second scenario, commences to concoct a special soup for his party, only to be surprised in the end by his mother's arrival with a cake. In the next story Little Bear launches an imaginary flight to the moon but returns to earth for lunchtime. And in the final episode Mother Bear puts Little Bear to sleep with a bedtime discussion and story.

Minarik thoughtfully works with the required repetition, making this limitation artful. She does so in three ways. First, in her sentences she achieves a lyrical rhythm by repeating phrases in the form of appositives and varied patterns. In *Little Bear* Mother Bear says, "See, Little Bear. I have something, something for my little bear."[10] Here Minarik uses the repetition of an appositive phrase that adds an endearing tone to Mother Bear's address to her son. Elsewhere, as in Little Bear's catalog of the pantry holdings for making his birthday soup, Minarik uses varied phrasing to make the most of the individual rhythm of the words themselves. "Let me see what we have," says Little Bear. "We have carrots and potatoes, peas and tomatoes; I can make soup with carrots, potatoes, peas and tomatoes" (*Little Bear*, 23).

Second, in creating individual episodes Minarik repeats parallel actions for humor. In *Little Bear* she narrates Little Bear's pestering of Mother Bear in word-for-word repetition. At each of Little Bear's entrances for another article of clothing, Minarik repeats, "Here is Little Bear" (14) and then "Here is Little Bear again" (16) and "Here is Little Bear again" (18). By speaking directly to the reader, she lets her or him in on the joke, as if in an aside, that Little Bear cannot be content. This type of repetition is also a favorite formula for joke telling in children's "knock knock" jokes, which can string together a whole series of repartees to build to a grand finale of a punch line. Minarik makes her joke by repeating Little Bear's appearance at Mother Bear's knee for something more to wear; then, for a punch line, Mother Bear removes each article of clothing she formerly gave him. In the end, all he is left wearing is his own fur coat (19–21).

Third, in her plots Minarik uses repetition for a framing device. She often has the animals tell stories-within-the-story. At the end of *Little Bear,* Mother Bear retells the whole book as her bedtime story for Little Bear. In reverse, at the beginning of *Little Bear's Friend* Little Bear retells the first chapter by telling Mother Bear all about his day, how he surveyed the countryside and met a new little girlfriend named Emily. Minarik is careful, however, not to overdo the technique. She devotes the rest of *Little Bear's Friend* to developing the variety of ways in which friends care for one another: Little Bear and Emily help Duck find a lost duckling; Little Bear mends Emily's broken doll; and when, finally, Emily leaves for the winter, she and Little Bear exchange good-byes and gifts. At the close of this last chapter, Little Bear pens Emily a letter. Here Minarik might again have employed a framing device, using Little Bear's letter as a reminiscence of the summer's past events; instead she focuses Little Bear's letter on the present ("It is snowing," he writes); and the future ("I cannot wait for summer")[11]—a closing that provided a good prompt for Minarik's next volume.

Minarik's most explicit use of a framing device comes in that ensuing book—*Little Bear's Visit*—in which Little Bear goes to visit his grandparents (chapter 1), they each tell him a story (chapters 2–3), and his parents return to bring him home (chapter 4). In short, what could have been redundant prose instead reads as a literary first reader, with varied styles of repetition.

In perfect bravado, Sendak aligns with Minarik's choice to make the utilitarian elegant by quoting from the historical period in art when that was one of the chief values: the nineteenth century. In the late 1800s William Morris elevated bookmaking to an art, not just an industry, a concern shared by Sendak. As part of the arts and crafts movement in England, Morris advocated that tools, furniture, or any other articles formerly designed only for practicality be decorated elegantly as well, for aesthetic pleasure. He then applied this principle to books. Using forms and shapes from nature—such as petals, tendrils, and birds—Morris arranged them geometrically into elaborate decorations in his books' margins. Earlier, in *Charlotte and the White Horse,* Sendak had designed endpapers with colorful vine, blossom, and tendril patterns; in the *Little Bear* books, however, he uses decoration holistically throughout each volume, both for a unified package and as an aesthetic parallel from volume to volume within the entire series.

On the cover of each book, Sendak frames the title and picture with an intricate, interlacing pattern of natural forms, using vines, branches, leaves, or tendrils. He has great fun with the concept of making the ordinary ornamental, especially on the cover for *Father Bear Comes Home.* To celebrate Little Bear's fisherman-father's return from sea, Minarik strings together three big fish stories—Little Bear fishes for an octopus, pretends his father caught a mermaid, and attempts to find a mermaid himself. Sendak designs the volume's cover appropriately: he draws curlicues to resemble hooks, lines, and sinkers; hangs whole fish from a hook in each corner; and tops off the effect with a centered illustration of Father Bear fishing from a rowboat at the moment of a catch.

In all five of the *Little Bear* books Sendak carefully decorates each page with a border, usually flourishing the design in each corner with a pattern of tendrils. Again using the ordinary for the ornamental, Sendak in the first volume's "Birthday Soup" chapter hangs three tomatoes, three potatoes, two carrots, and two pea pods from the tendrils in the border to dress up the page as a pantry, doing so with a minimum use of space. Underneath the hanging vegetables waits the black soup pot. Though the concept of using vegetables for designs is not original with him, in this illustration Sendak makes the effect his own.

Sendak's use of nineteenth-century influences works because he tastefully blends his style with Minarik's purpose. Minarik keeps her narrative simple for her early readers, and Sendak honors that simplicity by remaking the ornate Morrisian margins into elegantly lined edges with small flourishes in the corners.

Minarik's text and Sendak's illustrations work together because they both express the same spirit, a spirit of tenderness without being saccharine. Both achieve this quality through humor.

One of my favorite examples of Minarik's humor is her revolt against the sentimental in the last volume of the series, *A Kiss for Little Bear.* Of all the volumes, this one probably had the most potential for being mawkish, because of its impetus: Minarik, on discovering Sendak had suffered a major heart attack, decided for this volume to feature Little Bear as an artist, in tribute to her admired collaborator (Lanes, 144). In the story Little Bear sends a picture to his grandmother via Hen. His grandmother is so overjoyed that she wants to send Little Bear back a kiss. This kiss is passed from Hen to Frog, from Frog to Cat, and from Cat to Little Skunk, until the skunks begin to relish the passing of the kiss between them more than the passing of the kiss to Little Bear. When Little Skunk first receives the kiss from Cat, he spies another skunk. "She was very pretty," writes Minarik. "He gave the kiss to her. And she gave it back. And he gave it back. And then Hen came along. 'Too much kissing,' she said."[12] This episode epitomizes Minarik's response to sentimentality—she creates a wealth of affection but never overwrites the emotion.

In the same spirit Sendak manipulates his Victorian setting to express a tender humor inherent in Little Bear and his mother's relationship. Sendak says his choice focused on the type of femininity the Victorian age would offer Mother Bear: "Of course I wanted Mother Bear to be an image of warmth and strength— nothing less than motherhood itself. So I dressed her in Victorian costume, because those voluminous skirts, the voluminous sleeves, and her voluminous figure all made for the strong and comforting tenderness I wanted her to exude. And when Little Bear sat in her lap, I had her envelop him. The folds of her skirt surrounded him. There couldn't be a safer place in all the world than Mother Bear's lap" (Lanes, 53, 55). Sendak's portrait of Mother Bear is not only endearing but also roundly jolly. The conceit of a lumbering grizzly bear dressed in a stiff-necked collar with a brooch tight at her throat makes a satiric image of the ursine dressed up as the genteel. In this sense Sendak's illustrations caricature the nineteenth century, with its highly refined manners on the exterior yet its animal instincts poking out from underneath.

More explicitly humorous, and quoting from the works of two nineteenth-century artists, Sendak's illustrations mimic popular paintings of the time, making light of his own indebtedness to his Victorian wellspring. First, in *Father Bear* Sendak draws an illustration strongly suggestive of an inset from Georges Seurat's *Sunday Afternoon on the Island of La Grande Jatte* (1884–86). Though Sendak's couple is facing the water in the opposite direction from Seurat's pair, the composition of Mother and Father Bear closely resembles that of the gentleman and lady on the far right-hand side of Seurat's canvas. In similar design, both couples face toward the water, eyeing sailboats in the distance. Both Mother Bear and Seurat's lady strike similar poses, profiled by their parasols and bustles. Trees divide the background vertically in both pieces; grass lies at their feet. In similar attire, each hatted, Father Bear and Seurat's gentleman hold their respective umbrellas and walking sticks to the side, while both women sport milliner's ornaments on the fronts of their hats and wear dark blouses with lighter skirts. At the women's skirt tails, however, the humorous substitution in the parallel designs comes into view. Below each couple's knees scampers a small pet. And whereas Seurat has his lady holding the leash to a monkey, Sendak cleverly substitutes Little Bear, who, in testimony to his monkeying nature, is looking in the complete opposite direction from his parents.

Isolated from Seurat's inset, the illustration by Sendak works on its own for this very reason that Little Bear, while walking along with his parents, looks elsewhere. His waywardness creates the humor. But seen in contrast to Seurat's picture, the Bear family as a whole draws a laugh for their overreaching refinement, posing as the French on holiday.

Second, in *Kiss for Little Bear* Sendak caricatures the work of the nineteenth-century painter James Abbott McNeill Whistler more obviously. Sendak positions Grandmother Bear in the same profile with matching cap as Whistler's mother in his *Arrangement in Gray and Black No. 1 (The Artist's Mother)* (1871). Besides adding Hen to his arrangement, Sendak makes two meaningful substitutions from Whistler's piece. In place of the landscape hanging on Whistler's wall for geometric balance, Sendak hangs Little Bear's freehand drawing of a wild thing, thereby making a jab both at the high seriousness of Whistler and at his own art. The incongruence of the wild thing posted next to demure Grandmother Bear makes for a winning combination. And in place of Mother Whistler's icy stare, Sendak draws an open-jowled chuckle on his Grandmother Bear.

For the Little Bear series, Sendak does more than merely dress the three bears in Victorian attire. He uses the whole context of the nineteenth-century setting to create the most appropriate background for the charm and humor of Minarik's texts.

Collaboration with DeJong

Unlike Krauss and Minarik, Meindert DeJong writes junior novels for an older reading audience, children in the third through fifth grades. Consequently, Sendak adjusts his illustrating style to work with this genre. When illustrating the brief texts of Krauss and Minarik, Sendak can elaborate on the omitted details; his pictures, because they appear on almost every page, carry much of the responsibility of telling the story. For these junior novels, however, DeJong already provides the reader with detailed descriptions of plot, character, and setting, and he further elaborates on the motives, feelings, and mind-sets of his characters. His books average 150–300 pages each. For such lengthy texts, the desire of Sendak for his illustrations to "*vivify, quicken,* and *vitalize*" the text becomes crucial ("Shape of Music," 201). As Perry Nodelman writes in his *Words about Pictures,* "good black-and-white pictures that emphasize line over shape can add energy to long books in which details of emotion and of setting might otherwise retard the action."[13] Sendak, drawing only in pen-and-ink, captures the spirit of DeJong's novels in his illustrations and does indeed "add energy" to the stories through a progressively finer line.

Shadrach

A runner-up for the 1954 Newbery Medal and an ALA Notable Book, *Shadrach* (1953) is DeJong and Sendak's first junior novel together. Set in the Netherlands, the book tells the story of a young boy named Davie who, while recuperating from a severe illness, receives a rabbit, Shadrach. As Davie immerses himself in caring for his new pet, his family—mother, father, grandparents, and brother—watch him gain strength of character. For the first five chapters, DeJong describes Davie's anticipating the arrival of the rabbit; for the last five chapters, he describes the boy's care of his new pet. It is difficult for this central event of receiving a rabbit to sustain intensity over the book's 182 pages. Sendak thus adds energy to this lengthy narrative concerned with relatively minor domestic actions by illustrating those moments in the story when Davie experiences his most intense emotions.

When DeJong suggests Davie's ambivalent feelings toward members of his family, Sendak highlights the more significant emotion for the story through his illustrations. Often Davie will both hate and admire his older brother, Rem. At such points in the story Sendak selects the emotion that propels the story line forward. For example, when Rem discovers the lost Davie, who has wandered away to the dangerous dikes in search of clover for Shadrach, an episode follows in which Davie is described first as hotly angry at his brother and then as "big and proud" to get to walk beside him (*Shadrach,* 42), and here Sendak chooses to illustrate the moment compelling the latter sentiment. He pictures

Rem helping Davie outwit their parents. During his escapade Davie has accidentally slipped his feet into the dike, a misdemeanor Rem disguises by drying out his younger brother's socks (43). At this moment Davie, in a rare judgment, sees Rem as such "a good brother" (43). Sendak's choice to highlight Rem's empathizing with Davie helps move the story along because it foreshadows Rem's lying for Davie later in front of their furious parents. In this way too Sendak's illustration helps fully characterize Rem as a sympathetic figure here in the beginning, in contrast to his role as a mean tease at the end of the book.

Later in the story, when DeJong deliberates for 10 pages on Davie's ambivalent feelings toward his mother, Sendak highlights Davie's strongest emotion toward his mother and thereby keeps the story from getting bogged down. Davie is irritated with his mother for treating him like a baby and keeping him in bed; at the same time, he is sensitive to her worrying about him; and, to compound matters, he is also beginning to feel guilty toward her for not confessing that Rem has lied. To clarify Davie's muddled emotions, Sendak draws Davie hurriedly hugging his mother (55), thus presenting Davie's desire to love his mother as the sentiment dominating the emotional twists and turns in the narrative. Sendak's visual focus on Davie's overall love for his mother is necessary because the boy frequently seems to have mixed feelings toward his mother's disciplinary actions.

Besides keeping the story moving by clarifying important emotions from confusing passages, Sendak adds energy to the narrative by choosing to illustrate the scenes of strongest emotions. One of the most overwhelming scenes for Davie is the rainy day the rabbit actually arrives. With the rabbit finally in his arms, Davie loses all his reserve. "'Oh, Mom,' he [says] and it had to express all his great gratitude and all his excitement. 'Mom, can't we go faster?'" (97). In his picture Sendak illustrates both the content and the spirit of DeJong's passage. He pictures this moment when mother and son hurry home together in the rain (96). Interestingly, he sketches the two facing away from the reader; in this way his illustration does not show Shadrach, the new rabbit. By focusing on mother and son under the wide spread

of the umbrella, Sendak illuminates the spirit of intimacy experienced between mother and child. Under the slanting umbrella, Mother leans in toward Davie, resting her hand at the
nape of his neck. Sendak's contrast of her broad backside with
the boy's short frame captures a sense of the mother's security for
Davie.

At this point in his career, however, Sendak's draftsmanship is
uneven. Though most of the time Sendak accurately portrays the
same emotional tenor DeJong suggests in the text, at one point
he does not. In the last chapter Shadrach is missing; it is the
emotional nadir of the story. Then, eight pages from the end of
the book, Davie wakes up from his night's sleep and realizes
where Shadrach must be—in the barn. In the text, DeJong describes Davie's hopeful nighttime walk to the barn through emblems of clarity: "Outside the moon was shining cool and clear. It
lit the yard. It wasn't raining any more. On bare feet he went
across the cold wet yard to the barn. And everything in the moon-
lit night looked cold and clean and clear" (175). Sendak draws a
different picture. Although he does show Davie in his barefeet
and nightshirt walking in the moonlight to the barn, the scene is
blurred, not clear. Sendak makes marks across the moon's face,
almost as if it were still raining. He makes the shadows behind
Davie so dense that no clear shapes are discernible. The effect of
the illustration is surreal, as if Davie were befuddled rather than
sure. In Sendak's style, the tone of the illustration does not support DeJong's verbal description in the narrative.

This is an example of Sendak's earliest draftsmanship in which
the energy of the illustration's line is stifled by the busyness of
the background scenery. A busy background is not arbitrarily
right or wrong. But when the details of leaves and trees, roads
and horizons distract from the picture's main subject, then the
scenery saps the energy of the illustration.

A more widespread problem in Sendak's skill throughout *Shadrach* is the incongruous portraits of Davie and his family. Not all
of Sendak's portraits of a given character resemble one another.
Sendak draws Grandpa's features differently with almost each
illustration of him: on page 25, Grandpa has a Daumier-style

peasant face with wavy hair; on page 90, Grandpa's profile resembles the lines for a cartoon character's, and his hair texture has changed from slightly wavy to bushy. Moreover, Davie, on page 121, looks like Ernest Shepard's Christopher Robin; on page 156, he resembles one of Sendak's own scamps from *Open House,* appearing eight years later.

Hurry Home, Candy

Sendak's technical skill continues to lack refinement in his next collaboration with DeJong, *Hurry Home, Candy* (1953). Like her human counterpart Oliver Twist, Candy, a lost dog who becomes a stray for a year, keeps finding security but then immediately faces a calamity that displaces her once again. Candy runs scared from the beginning of the novel to its close. As DeJong writes, "The little dog's memory began in fear" (*Candy,* 19). While still a nursing puppy, Candy is wrenched from her mother to be the pet of young Catherine and her brother, George. The children play gently with their new puppy, but their parents frighten Candy, especially by using a broom on her. Consequently, brooms become powerful symbols of fear for Candy throughout the novel.

During a family outing it is in fact a broom that causes Candy to become separated from Catherine. While the family is stopped on a bridge overhead to repair a flat tire, Catherine and Candy explore the creek below. Suddenly a hailstorm pours down. As Catherine scrambles up the bank for the car, Candy is frozen in place by a broom in her path. In her hesitation she loses Catherine.

Henceforward Candy experiences a succession of hardships. A pack of dogs chases her under a pig farmer's wagon. The pig farmer offers a respite from hunger and loneliness; then, injured in an accident, the farmer leaves Candy in the custody of the police and pound. There Candy fares well until she inadvertently encounters a broom and runs away. Just as the kind gentleman Mr. Brownlow rescues Oliver Twist from the streets, Captain Carlson rescues Candy and takes her home. For one week, Carlson and his home are "heaven" to Candy (173); however, in a bizarre turn of events, Candy—at the same bridge where she was separated from

Catherine—is forced from Carlson by a police-robber shoot-out. Wounded and lost, she stumbles on Catherine and George's grandparents' house. But because she will not return to that family, the grandparents make it possible for her to be reunited in the end with Captain Carlson.

Sendak's drawing of the brooms in the story epitomizes his awkward draftsmanship at this point in his career. Although DeJong uses the broom as the powerful motive for Candy's fear throughout the narrative, Sendak renders it inconsequentially— in stick fashion with toylike dimensions. At the book's finale, when happiness at last seems in store for Candy in Carlson's home, DeJong prolongs the suspense by blocking Candy's path one more time with a broom. As the dog approaches Carlson's back door, she spies a broom left there unknowingly by the cleaning woman. Carlson realizes the situation just in time to hurl the broom out of Candy's way and into a pine tree, signaling his unreserved welcome of Candy. In his potentially poignant final illustration juxtaposing the broom and Carlson's wide-open door, Sendak executes the broom caught in the tree in physically impossible detail (243), plastering the vertical broom almost perpendicularly against the horizontal pine branches and thereby creating a visual distraction from DeJong's salient detail in the narrative. And in Sendak's illustration for Candy's initial separation from Catherine, he pictures the broom in toylike dimensions rather than as a threatening image for Candy (67).

The same lack of distinction between background and subject that marred *Shadrach* spoils the illustrations for *Candy* as well. Sendak uses scribbled, dense lines to serve as background mass, color, shadow, and foliage. Using backgrounds in almost every illustration, he crowds the drawings with trees and details that, while expressing the dark, naturalistic tone of DeJong's narrative, also weaken the dynamics of the images.

Further, in his illustration of Candy's initial separation from Catherine during the hailstorm (67), Sendak selects this dramatic moment for a potentially dynamic illustration. Unfortunately, however, the denseness of line in his scenery smothers the alacrity of Catherine, who is the source of energy for the episode. DeJong describes Catherine with electrifying drama: "She started running from under the bridge, tore up the steep gully. But the gully had become slippery with rain. She tripped, fell flat. She screamed but blindly scrambled up again. The old broom slid down beside her. Whimpering with fear, she struggled up the gully. The rain water gushed down" (67). In Sendak's illustration Catherine appears stiff and lifeless against the bank. Though his dense lines capture the menace of the storm, rather than spur the narrative forward they halt the reader to search for Catherine's drama lost in the busy design.

The Wheel on the School

Only a year later, and after his first excursion to Europe, Sendak's prowess improved markedly. For DeJong's *The Wheel on the School* (1954), winner of the 1955 Newbery Medal, Sendak illustrates in the same vigorous spirit as DeJong narrates. Sendak pictures the tension between DeJong's Dutch villagers and their fierce climate in a masterful way. Omitting background scenery, he isolates the human figures to let their physical postures suggest the cold, windy setting. Adding a wash to his work, Sendak creates the extra value of gray for his pen-and-ink illustrations. The gray flexibly connotes water, fog, and wind; more important, it allows Sendak the space to vivify the lines in his pictures. This time, Sendak's illustrations delineate the resilient temper of DeJong's Hollanders.

Wheel tells the story of seven schoolchildren's dream to bring storks back to their village. Their teacher encourages them to realize this dream by first wondering why their seaside village of Shora has no storks, "for when we wonder," he tells them, "we can make things begin to happen."[14] The rest of the book tells the children's adventures in luring back the storks. Just as their fishermen-fathers face the wind and the waves, the children confront nature's harshness in the story. Yet through their fortitude, they also learn of nature's beauty as they watch, in the end, a male and female stork begin to make their nest on the village school's rooftop.

Sendak's isolation of the figures is especially powerful during the storm chapter. By omitting any background, he suggests the desolate setting for DeJong's narrative. In the accompanying passage DeJong writes, "Somewhere out there in the deep of night were voices screaming on the dike. People yelled at each other against the thunder of the waves and wind. The wind made voices sound hopeless and helpless—like the cries of a wounded animal" (*Wheel,* 189–90). Here at the chapter heading, Sendak, using pen-and-ink with a wash, draws only three bulky figures stooped into the wind. Rather than crowding the illustration with many bodies, which might weaken the episode's energy, Sendak lets his three figures stand for the many out on the dike. He does so by drawing them facing away, their facelessness suggesting that they could be anyone and everyone. And in his simple yet sophisticated design, he uses the upturned lines of skirt tails to suggest the rush in the women's steps.

Farther into the chapter Sendak draws two companion illustrations of the villagers bent into the wind, women on one page, men on the other (200–1). Again without using any background scenery, Sendak suggests the gusty wind and frigid temperature through the body postures of the characters. The women clutch the shawls at their throats and lean forward on one foot, as if running. The men's shoulders bend forward, saddling their heavy figures with worry. In *Wheel* Sendak employs much less detail than in *Shadrach* or *Hurry Home, Candy,* but he illustrates much more. He captures the perseverance of the fishing families in DeJong's Holland.

The House of Sixty Fathers

In 1956 Sendak collaborated with DeJong on *The House of Sixty Fathers,* a difficult book to illustrate for children, in that the story involves the grimness of life for a child during World War II.[15] DeJong tells the story of Tien Pao, a Chinese boy who becomes separated from his parents and baby sister and finds himself in Japanese-occupied territory. In pursuit of his family, Tien Pao experiences hunger, gunfire, and loneliness—he has only a pig for a companion. Thinking himself a war orphan, he finds himself miraculously fathered by a whole barrackful of 60 American soldiers. Through their effort and support, he is ultimately reunited with his Chinese family.

In illustrating this novel Sendak locates the energy for the pictures not in the draining subjects of battles and bombs but in the motivating strength behind Tien Pao's endurance—the search for his family. Sendak chooses to picture scenes from DeJong's text that together create a visual narrative of the boy finding a sister, father, mother, and even home for the ones he lost. In this way Sendak highlights the main story within DeJong's longer account. He directs the reader not to dwell on the myriad details during Tien Pao's journey but instead to follow the distinct motif of family. This aspect is important for the 189-page novel because DeJong's story of Tien Pao is unavoidably complicated. Tien Pao is lost in the mountains for days; by the time the American soldiers find him, he is unconscious. Rather than depict the physical details that keep Tien Pao going—eating leaves and hiding in caves—Sendak selects those human beings in the midst of the war who keep the young boy's spirit hopeful.

In close empathy with the text, Sendak selects moments for illustration that hinge on this war child's need for a family. DeJong sets up a correspondence in the text between Tien Pao's real family and his makeshift one. Sendak illuminates this correspondence by picturing Tien Pao with each member of this new surrogate family. Humorously, DeJong sets up Tien Pao's pet pig as a substitute for his baby sister; whereas his sister is named Beauty-of-the-Republic, Tien Pao renames his pet Glory-of-the-Republic after her (*Sixty,* 33). Sendak highlights this substitution by picturing Tien Pao holding the pig protectively (32), paralleling an earlier illustration of him shielding his sister protectively (5).

In chapter 4, "The River Cliff," Sendak stresses Tien Pao finding a father figure. This chapter recounts Tien Pao's witnessing of the air raid on the Japanese soldiers and then the crash of the American plane. Tien Pao and Glory-of-the-Republic run for their lives away from the Japanese bullets to find the wounded pilot. To accompany this trauma, Sendak uses three illustrations: a Japanese soldier with rifle cocked (58), four Japanese soldiers running (65), and Tien Pao seated on the lap of Lieutenant Hamsun (74). By not picturing Tien Pao in any of the scenes of Japanese soldiers, Sendak's illustrations separate Tien Pao from the bloodshed. Sendak couches the young boy on the safe lap of the reclining pilot. From the picture, the pilot does not even look like a soldier; his uniform coat is off and his shirt collar unbuttoned. Alone with the boy, the lieutenant appears a smiling father to him.

This illustration foreshadows the main conceit of the book referred to by the title, that a whole troop of American soldiers will adopt Tien Pao as their ward. Sendak, however, is careful to illustrate that the transfer of Tien Pao's familial affection from his own father to the American soldiers is not easily made for the boy. Later in the story Sendak pictures an aloof Tien Pao in the foreground, staring at faceless soldiers in the background (164). Although this picture accompanies that part of the story which marks the joyous reunion of Tien Pao with Lieutenant Hamsun, the wide white space between Tien Pao and the lieutenant in the picture works emblematically to suggest how emotionally distant Tien Pao feels from the foreign man.

In the narrative the boy and his airman are separated in the chapter following their first encounter. It is significant, then, that in this chapter (chapter 5, "Cuckoos Call at Night") DeJong and Sendak present a mother figure for Tien Pao. When Chinese guerilla mountain soldiers take in the boy, DeJong presents one of the men's wives as if she were Tien Pao's mother. She has the same name as his mother—Yin—and, to Tien Pao, even resembles her (96). The guerilla leader says explicitly to Tien Pao, "This is your mother while we are here" (96). Likewise, Sendak emphasizes the young woman as a mother to Tien Pao in one of the novel's most beautiful illustrations. In fine lines he draws the woman bending over the boy in a basin, bathing him. The composition is balanced in a triangular design. Three dark shadings form each corner of the triangle: the woman's black hair in a bun, the black crescent of the bathwater, and the blackness of Tien Pao's turned head. Sendak uses delicate lines to delineate rounded, womb shapes: the bend of the woman's broad back, the circle of her bun, the curve of the basin, and even Tien Pao's squatting position. Crosshatching over the woman's face, leaving her featureless, Sendak allows her to be for this moment the boy's own mother (99).

It is important to note that by highlighting Tien Pao's search for his family members, Sendak does not censor the rest of the text. He pictures the starving children who eat mud and grass; he pictures the Japanese soldiers; he pictures the Chinese refugees, homeless in their own land. But when he pictures Tien Pao, he often pictures him with his pig or an American soldier and once with the maternal Yin. Sendak's choice to isolate the human figures, as he did for *Wheel,* presents war as a personal tragedy rather than as an abstract political event.

Conclusion

Some critics view Sendak's illustrations in the fifties and early sixties as better than those in the eighties, such as the illustrations in the later *Outside Over There.* Writes Geraldine DeLuca, "One sees art that is much closer to the spirit of childhood, to the vulnerability Sendak so often mentions, the freshness, the honesty and directness."[16] She further posits that this simpler liveliness of Sendak's earlier pictures as a whole may stem from the freedom he felt to collaborate with writers before he became responsible for both words and pictures in his later books (DeLuca 1986, 147).

I believe that Sendak's style, especially for Krauss's texts, was "lighter" because the narratives he worked with were carefree. During Sendak's early collaborations, he experimented with a wide variety of styles—for DeJong's novels alone he employed a mixture of cartoon and realistic drawings, pen-and-ink wash, and even some techniques from pointillism for *Sixty Fathers.* The sequence of his developing style for DeJong's novels attests to the fact that the cartoon characters who suited Krauss's texts perfectly did not always match the moodier tone of, for example, *Candy.* Likewise, Sendak's anthropomorphic approach to illustrating Minarik's Little Bear family would have been ludicrous for picturing Tien Pao's pig. In short, Sendak seems to have been experimenting not with simply finding a style that worked across the board for any collaborator but with sensitively learning how to tailor-make each assignment he undertook with the most apt style for that particular narrative.

More than any isolated style, achieving a harmony between the tone of the text and the mood of the picture is the most striking standard Sendak established during his early career. Based on that criterion, his collaborative work with Krauss is probably some of the best in his canon, as DeLuca intimates. With Krauss more than with Minarik or DeJong, Sendak is allowed more liberty to influence the storytelling. Given that opportunity, he exhibits a talent for pictorial narrative. The briefer the text, the more powerful Sendak's pictures become in terms of shaping the story, embellishing its details, and providing its motives. His aptitude for collaborating with brief texts was a working situation Sendak had to relearn when it came time to illustrate his own narratives.

Given the high standard that words and pictures tell a book's story together and in the same spirit, Sendak's style has thus developed into one as fluid and changeable as the texts he has illustrated. Incredibly, it is the same Sendak who designed both the tiny, tight pen-and-ink landscapes for Randall Jarrell's *Animal Family* and the squalling portrait of the ugly baby for Frank Stockton's *Bee-Man of Orn*. The tones, lines, and color of the illustrations are completely different because the spirit of the texts are as well. Sendak's style has become as varied as the narratives he illustrates.

3

Early Books: Signaling Make-Believe

After illustrating for other writers, Sendak in 1956 turned to illustrating his own books, starting with *Kenny's Window*. Six other books followed in quick succession: *Very Far Away* (1957), *The Sign on Rosie's Door* (1960), and *The Nutshell Library* (1962), including the individual volumes of *Alligators All Around, Chicken Soup with Rice, One Was Johnny,* and *Pierre.* With these seven works Sendak staked his claim to write about children playing make-believe. As a budding fantasist, Sendak faced the artistic problem of how to "solidify" the ideas for his books about fantasy into "a palpable shape" so that they "[meant] something to somebody else."[1] He had to make stylistic choices about how to indicate through his illustrating techniques and now through his language that his characters were engaged in imaginative play.

Graphic Devices to Suggest Fantasy

In his book *Words about Pictures* Perry Nodelman describes the style of Sendak's art in his early books as "close to the commonplace conventions of most cartoons" (78). There Sendak sometimes resorts to stereotypical devices often found in comic strips when his transitions from the ordinary world to the fanciful one occur abruptly in his text.

One of his devices is both obvious and successful: to indicate that a character is pretending, Sendak literally dresses him or her to play the part. Interestingly, in the eighteenth century the word "disguise" could be used to mean a make-believe game played by children. Thus, in Blake's short poem "Nurses Song" the killjoy governess marshalls her charges indoors for the evening with the reprimand "Your spring & your day are wasted in play, / And your winter and night in disguise."[2] When Sendak's twentieth-century children play pretend, they literally sport "disguises." In *Very Far Away* Martin dons a cowboy hat and false mustache "so no one would recognize him"; in *The Sign on Rosie's Door* Rosie adorns herself as Alinda, "the lovely lady singer," complete with boa, evening gloves, and low-cut dress to entertain her friends. Even in *Alligators All Around* the reptile family "disguise" themselves as "Indians" and lions. These early costumes set the precedent for Max's famous "wolf suit," Mickey's doughy aviator outfit, and Ida's yellow rain cloak. In short, Sendak found a device that worked from the beginning for signaling the onset of fantasy play; other devices were not as successful.

Sendak's early means of illustrating memories in the stories serve as prime examples. *Kenny's Window,* the story of a young boy who stays in his room daydreaming, opens with Kenny remembering a dream in which a rooster gave him seven questions to answer; for the rest of the book, Kenny busies himself in seven different sketches exploring an answer for a question with his teddy bear, wooden soldiers, and pet terrier named Baby. When Baby recalls for Kenny the time she thought she was an elephant, Sendak illustrates the memory literally in the accompanying picture. He draws an elephant in Kenny's bedroom. To clarify that this elephant is simply a figment of Baby's (or actually Kenny's) imagination, Sendak renders the elephant in a tentative line and translucent color, outlining its shape with a dotted line and then superimposing its lighter cream image over Baby's black-and-white one. In contrast, he distinguishes Baby and her bone as elements of the real world by defining their forms in black.

In *Very Far Away* the abrupt time change from present to distant past elicits another convention from Sendak in the illustrations. In this story Martin, unable to get his mother's attention, runs away to a hideout he calls "very far away." Equally unhappy with their present situations, a horse, sparrow, and cat join the boy. One by one, each malcontent tells his or her story of better days until an argument breaks out and the group disbands. Somewhat consoled, Martin returns home. Here Sendak limits the reveries of each character to one page. In the illustrations he uses the cartoon device of insets above the respective characters' heads to set their daydreams apart from Martin's everyday setting (*Very Far Away*, 36–41).

In Sendak's early works his movement from the everyday world to the imaginary one or vice versa often occurs so suddenly that he is forced to use overt divisions in the already-short narratives. To accommodate such splices in the narrative, Sendak will illustrate the entire change of setting in a single page turn. This type of sudden transition appears most blatantly in *Kenny's Window,* which, characteristic of Sendak's early works, is divided into brief sections, in this case eight, with the first section serving as an introduction. In the second section Sendak uses an abrupt transition for Kenny's imaginary trip from home to the Swiss Alps. He writes, "Kenny left a note on the kitchen table. It said: Dear mama, Am going to Switzerland. Back soon. Kenny. The valleys of Switzerland were deep in wild flowers." The accompanying picture omits any transition for the change in setting; the viewer flips from a picture of Kenny's drawing of his teddy bear riding a rooster to a picture of Kenny standing in a mountain meadow. In comic strips this type of disjointed sequence from one frame to the next is sometimes labeled with an extra caption similar to the standby "Meanwhile, back at the ranch." Sendak adopts such a strategy for *Very Far Away,* labeling Martin's new setting in his fantasy world with an inserted title page reading "Book 2 VERY FAR AWAY" (33).

What's significant about Sendak's developed sense of transition in the later picture-book trilogy is that he did not resort to such abruptly imposed transitions. After he learned to write gradual transitions in his texts, his illustrations unfolded the fantasies gradually as well. He began to use a series of pictures rather than

a single, often-jarring switch from one world to the next. For example, Sendak gives Max six pages of text and six illustrations to
get to where the wild things are; he devotes nine frames to getting
Mickey into the night kitchen; and he uses nine illustrations to
weave Ida's journey to "outside over there." Because Sendak allows so much space and distance between the characters' ordinary worlds and their imagined ones, he does not need to use
dotted lines or insets to enclose the make-believe scenes. In this
way he frees himself to create the memorable images of the wild
things, the Oliver-Hardy bakers, and the goblin babies. By using
solid lines and bold colors for the fantasies in the picture books,
Sendak suggests fantasy worlds as palpable as the children's
everyday worlds.

Passive to Active Syntax

From the onset of his career, Sendak viewed his role as an illustrator as a collaborative one with the writer. "I know that I would
not be an illustrator without words," he says (Lanes, 232). It follows, then, that after creating captivating pictures for the sea-
soned texts of Krauss, Minarik, DeJong, and others, Sendak could
not at first produce distinguished pictures for his own books, because he was struggling with his own writing style. He concedes
that writing is the more difficult medium for him but is the one
he must master first. He feels compelled to have a polished text
before designing its pictures: "My own texts have to be very good,
as far as I'm concerned, before I illustrate them," he explains
(Lanes, 232). Understandably, then, the rougher narratives of
Sendak's first books account partly for the poorer quality of his
pictures therein.

   Sendak describes *Kenny's Window* as "overwritten" (Commire,
27: 187) yet confesses that the pleasure he derives from the book
is "from staring back over a long career and sympathetically eyeing the first work that fumblingly—even hastily—set out all the
themes of one's lifetime, as if for a sumptuous but too ample dinner" (*Blechman*, 7). The delicacy of the narrative style in *Kenny's*

Window is only now discernible in view of the full spread of Sendak's works. An even closer review reveals that, besides the similar themes, some of Sendak's later stylistic merits come from techniques piloted in this book. In particular, Sendak's style in *Kenny's Window* offers a foretaste of his lean style in *Where the Wild Things Are.*

Sendak's narrative style in *Kenny's Window* may have developed into his narrative style for *Wild Things* because both books confront similar conflicts. The central problem of both *Kenny's Window* and *Wild Things* stems from the passive roles both Kenny and Max assume. In each story's beginning the main character is overwhelmed by feelings and situations seemingly outside his control; in each book the boy regains command of himself by actively fantasizing solutions. Strikingly, Sendak signals both boys' shift of attitude from passive to active in their imaginary world by means of his syntax.

Linguist Charles J. Fillmore posits that a writer's stylistic choices can express his judgment about the subject. Fillmore developed a method for the reader to decipher the writer's judgment by analyzing his syntax; he calls the method "role structure analysis" because it provides a means for determining the roles nouns play according to syntactic structure.[3] Fillmore discerns several role types, two of them—the Agent and the Patient—especially pertinent here.

Fillmore proposes that if a writer uses the active voice for her or his subject, she or he purposely presents the subject as taking an active role; thus, in the sentence "Schweitzer played the organ" Fillmore would label "Schweitzer" an Agent. Likewise, if a writer uses the passive voice in regard to his subject, as in the sentence "Mary Queen of Scots was executed," Fillmore would label "Mary" a Patient because the writer portrays Mary as being acted on rather than exerting her own command of the situation.

Fillmore's role labels serve as descriptive tools for the reader to grasp the experiences of Sendak's earliest protagonist—Kenny—and his later one—Max. Though Kenny and Max act predominantly in the assertive role of Agent, a close look at the opening patterns of syntax in each narrative reveals that it is the contrast between their roles of Patient and Agent that compels each fantasy forward.

The fact that in *Kenny's Window* the whole story takes place with Kenny alone in his bedroom indicates the boy's introvertedness. Sendak opens the story with Kenny sitting on his bed daydreaming and ends the book with Kenny still dreaming in bed. In the story Kenny does not change his personality; however, he does progress from the role of passive dreamer to that of a boy who can initiate his own dreams. Sendak mirrors this switch in Kenny's inner experience in his syntax.

As most good introductions do, Sendak's foreshadows the overall movement of the story, from the passive role Kenny plays in seeking his happiness to the active one he plays at the end. On the first page of text, Kenny awakens from a dream and describes what he recalls: "There was a tree covered white with blossoms. And above the tree shone the sun and the moon side by side. Half the garden was filled with yellow morning and the other with dark green night." With respect to Fillmore's role structure analysis, in this memory of his dream Kenny is not yet the central Agent, either syntactically or literally.

At this point in the story, Kenny is not engaged in discovering how to seek his own happiness; as is reflected metaphorically in the grammar, the dream seems to happen to Kenny, beyond his control. Sendak intensifies the sense of passivity by studding the passage just quoted with passive syntax. Three times on the page Sendak uses the expletive "there was," casting the sentences in the passive voice. Twice Sendak uses passive syntax, first in "a tree covered" and next in "the garden was filled." At the end of the page, however, Sendak challenges Kenny's passivity by introducing the queer, four-legged rooster who spurs Kenny to take charge and "find all the answers."

When the reader turns the page, the setting abruptly changes from inside Kenny's dream world to outside it, in his bedroom. Sendak has Kenny recall the same dream imagery, yet this time Sendak uses active syntax in the narrative, presenting Kenny squarely as Agent in his fantasy. Now Kenny says, "It would be nice to live in such a garden. In the morning I could sit in the nighttime half of the garden and count the stars and at night I could play in the morning-half of the garden and I'd never have to go to sleep. I'll find the answers to the seven questions." Though he begins Kenny's first sentence with the conditional construction "It would be," in the rest of the sentences Sendak uses the active voice, presenting Kenny as an instigator. Kenny pictures himself sitting, counting, playing, and staying up all night. This new image of himself is so appealing that Kenny resolves to become involved with his dream and "find the answers." Like Sally and her brother in *The Cat in the Hat,* Kenny learns to overcome boredom through an active imagination.

What it takes Sendak paragraphs to accomplish in *Kenny's Window* he later accomplishes in one sentence in *Wild Things.* In this picture book Sendak polishes the delicate detail of switching from the active to the passive voice to signal a change in Max's experience.

Sendak presents the tension in Max's experience when he suddenly changes Max from his initial role of Agent to that of Patient. In the opening sentence Sendak establishes this conflict through his syntax. He writes,

> The night Max wore his wolf suit and made mischief
> of one kind
> and another
> his mother called him "WILD THING!"
> and Max said "I'LL EAT YOU UP!"
> so he was sent to bed without eating anything.

From this introduction, the main conflict appears to be between Max and his mother. He yells at her and she sends him to his room. The syntax, however, reveals more about Max's experience when he gets punished. Using active verbs, Sendak presents Max as Agent—Max wears his wolf suit and makes mischief—and thus places Max in control of his own actions. Yet after Max shouts at his mother, Sendak presents Max as Patient being acted on when he says Max "was sent to bed." Sendak's use of the passive verb draws attention to the heart of the conflict between Max and his mother: Max loses control. He is being controlled by his mother, by the situation, and, most deeply, by his own hurt feelings. The need for Max to gain control of himself proves to be the drive behind the rest of the story.

Fairy-Tale Plots

In retrospect, Sendak's alteration of syntax from the passive to the active voice in *Kenny's Window* signaled the realm of fantasy in a significant way. It directed the movement of the book, and those to follow, into the archetypal shape of a fairy tale. In his book *The Uses of Enchantment* (1976) Bruno Bettelheim analyzes the shape of a fairy tale into specific beginning, middle, and closing episodes, which he describes as follows:

1. the hero becomes helpless
2. he goes on a quest
3. he masters himself and his situation[4]

Bettelheim's outline of the fairy tale parallels Sendak's framework for expressing Kenny's story. Sendak frames Kenny as initially passive, then actively searching for answers, and finally satisfied with the imaginative answers he creates. For Bettelheim, the benefit of such a fairy tale is derived from the cathartic opportunity it affords young readers to work vicariously through their own troubles (Bettelheim 1976, 158). This paradigm serves as the core plot for almost all the stories in the Sendakian canon.

In *Very Far Away* and *One Was Johnny* Sendak began repeating versions of Bettelheim's paradigm to indicate when the characters' make-believe play begins and ends. Sendak re-creates a version of Bettelheim's fairy-tale structure in Martin's make-believe search for "very far away." At the beginning of the story, Martin is helpless to make his mother pay attention to him; that is the reality of his everyday situation. Following Bettelheim's sequence of events, Martin leaves in search of a place "where somebody will answer [his] questions" (*Very Far Away*, 10). With this point of departure, Sendak begins Martin's imaginative play. As noted earlier, Martin initiates the play by disguising himself as a cowboy. The farther he wanders on his quest, the farther he removes himself from reality. As his fantasy develops, animals begin to talk and listen to him. Later, at Martin's farthest point from reality, these animals begin to share their own daydreams.

At the turning point of the story, Sendak restages an episode that parallels Martin's initial one with his mother. The animals no longer want to listen to one another or to Martin. At this point Martin literally and figuratively grows "disenchanted" with his make-believe play. Sendak uses this disenchantment to begin the transition from Martin's make-believe play back to his everyday world. The talking animals disband one by one, and Martin follows, resigning himself to his situation at home. He concedes that "if Mama's *still* not finished I'll sit on the steps and count automobiles while I wait" (50). Sendak ends the fantasy by illustrating Martin running home to his mother.

In this, Sendak's second version of a fairy-tale formula, the effect of a single quest out and back is neater than that of the disjointed, episodic structure of *Kenny's Window* but is nonetheless dissatisfying. Martin does not actually master himself or his situation, as called for in Bettelheim's scheme. As Selma Lanes points out, Martin does not face his own anger at the turning point; consequently, the story lacks a definite sense of resolution (Lanes, 75). Still, with *Very Far Away* Sendak does find a device in the quest version of the fairy tale that he will later develop into the fanciful journeys of Max, Mickey, and Ida.

In one of the slim *Nutshell* volumes, *One Was Johnny,* a book that counts up to 10 and then back down to 1, Sendak uses another version of Bettelheim's paradigm, a version I describe as "palindromic." A palindrome is a phrase or sentence that reads the same forward and backward, as in the famous examples "Madam, I'm Adam," by James Joyce, and "Doc, note. I dissent. A fast never prevents a fatness. I diet on cod," by Penelope Gilliatt. In *One Was Johnny* Sendak loosely follows such a forward-and-backward pattern to signal when make-believe play begins and ends. Corresponding to the ascending and descending count, Sendak sets up a series of events in a certain order for the first half of the narrative, offers the character a turning point, and then reverses the order of like events in the narrative's second half. Even in this brief narrative, Sendak improves on his fairy-tale structure in two ways: he uses it to create a problem to be solved, and he emphasizes its turning point as the climax for the book. Sendak begins the narrative with the line "1 was Johnny who lived by himself." This situation is Johnny's realistic arrangement; nothing out of the ordinary is happening, and Sendak pictures Johnny alone, reading a book. Then with each successive count, Sendak disrupts Johnny's calm repose with the entry of an uninvited guest, each type of intruder growing more and more farfetched. On the following page, a yellow rat springs in through Johnny's window as Sendak narrates, "2 was a rat who jumped on his shelf." On the count of 3, a cat springs after the rat. Next comes a dog, and then a turtle. But by the count of 10, Johnny's room has become crowded with less common guests—a monkey, a bird, a tiger, and a robber. With such a progression, Sendak intensifies Johnny's fantasy as it develops.

Sendak then focuses Johnny's problem as a question to the reader: "10 was a puzzle. What should Johnny do?" Moreover, he emphasizes this turning point in the palindromic pattern as the climax of the book by refraining from using an illustration. Instead, using a double spread of text, he enlarges the lettering to suggest metaphorically Johnny's augmented volume as he shouts his answer: "Here's what I'll do—I'll start to count backwards and when I am through—if this house isn't empty I'll eat all of you!!!!" Here Johnny masters his situation. His resolve sets in motion the series of departures that will return his situation to normal. Such a symmetrical narrative foreshadows the artistry of *Wild Things,* whose structure one critic described as "chiasmic."[5]

Pictorial Puns and Word Play

Sendak extends the careful craftsmanship of *One Was Johnny* to his other *Nutshell* books. Masterfully, he transforms their didactic formats for teaching numbers, letters, months, and a moral into pure entertainment. In this pint-size library Sendak creates metaphors interdependent on narrative and pictures. The playful dynamics between *Nutshell*'s illustrations and its narratives signal a realm of fantasy for the whole collection. Like a Pennsylvania Dutchman posting hexes on his barn, Sendak uses his book designs to ward off stodgy attitudes and to welcome imaginative ones.

Sendak puns on the "library's" reduced size as a metaphor for its character. In design, the library's structure parallels that of a nut, whose shell serves as a casing for the meat inside; here Sendak uses the snug slipcover to hold the four books—the "meat" of the library—in place. Punning with the title on the colloquial expression "in a nutshell" (that is, in the most concise form), Sendak fashions the four volumes in miniature: each tiny red book measures 3 ⅞ inches tall, 2 ¾ inches wide, and a mere ⅜ inch thick, the four of them fitting into a slipcase about 4 inches tall, 3 inches wide, and only 2 inches thick, slightly larger than a deck of cards.

Sendak decorates the slipcase with visual images that further pun on the library's contents. He designs the three side panels to suggest a Victorian wooden stage, and indeed each little book performs an act in itself, whether counting to ten, chanting the alphabet, rhyming the months, or dramatizing a moral. In his illustrations of the stage Sendak places two masks of comedy at the base of the columns, thus barring any tragedy from the play; at the top of the columns he places acorns—not only literally denoting the title but also connoting the library's "nutty," or crazy, subjects. On the top panel he draws a larger acorn with a crown at its tip and a garland of oak leaves at its base, the image of the crown making a pun on its placement at the "crown," or top, of the library and also metaphorically suggesting that *The Nutshell Library* is the "crowning" achievement of Sendak's canon at that time.

Sendak uses the side panels to preview the appearances of the principal characters—Pierre, the lion, a soup eater, and an alligator. He also chooses to include animals that emblematically characterize the books' contents. He pictures a monkey, which may well suggest the "monkey business" throughout the volumes. In *Alligators All Around*—an alphabet illustrated completely in alligators—the reptiles gad about "bursting balloons" and "entertaining elephants." Sendak also pictures the supporting actors of the cat and the rat from *One Was Johnny,* perhaps thus suggesting the featured cat-and-mouse games throughout the library; Pierre's disappearance into the lion's belly might even be classified by such a motif. In addition, Sendak's choice to picture the terrier on the library's front panel might well signal the "doggerel" verse inside that enhances the collection's lightheartedness.

Indeed, in contrast to the dense, random rhythm of the prose in Sendak's former books, the brief narratives in *Nutshell* are all written in rhymes and bouncy rhythms. Sendak's use of such rhythm serves a specific artistic purpose in *Pierre*. In this story Sendak's infamous, defiant Pierre refuses all his parents' requests. Then one day a lion asks Pierre "if he'd like to die" (*Nutshell,* 28). Pierre retorts that he does not care; consequently, the lion eats him (34). After being miraculously retrieved, Pierre recants his rebellious attitude. Because the tale warns its readers against a particular social misbehavior, Sendak adopts the rhythm traditionally used for lightly satiric verse and employs the scheme of the limerick. He writes the story's prologue in the conventional limerick pattern, using five anapestic lines of three feet in the rhyming first, second, and fifth lines and two feet in the rhyming third and fourth lines. For the story of *Pierre,* Sendak switches to iambic tetrameter but retains the characteristic anapestic meter of limericks for Pierre's repeated line *"I don't care!"* Here, not only do the words of Pierre go against his parents' wishes, but their meter differs from that of his parents' speech. At the close of the story, when Pierre mends his ways and minds his manners, Sendak changes the meter of his speech to be iambic like his parents'. In a reversal of his ways, signaled by the reversed metrical foot, Pierre shouts, *"Yes, indeed I care!!"* (46). The attention Sendak pays to the rhythm in *Pierre* foreshadows his use of syncopated rhythm in the picture books discussed at length in chapter 6. In those books Sendak begins to switch his metrical style at specific points in the stories to control the more disturbing episodes.

In addition to the puns on the slipcase's outside, Sendak continues his wordplay on *Nutshell*'s insides. In *One Was Johnny* he makes a visual pun of the "still," or quiet, life Johnny leads by arranging a "still life"—a bowl of fruit next to a lamp—on Johnny's table. Later, of course, the bowl of fruit provides an opportunity for a rhyme (and a crime), when Sendak counts down from seven to six in the lines "7 the blackbird flew off to Havana" and "6 was the monkey who stole a banana." The implied pun at the end of *Pierre* is the royal treatment the lion receives from the family, when they "lionize" their honored beast and host him as a "weekend guest" (48). By far the most explicit pun Sendak makes is with the title *Alligators All Around,* in which he uses the phrase "all around" prepositionally to suggest that the alligators get about to all sorts of places. In fact, the title page in the text features the whole family dressed up in hats and coats for an outing. The pun, however, is that the adjective "all-around" means "versatile" or "able to do many things," which is exactly how Sendak pictures these creatures. They juggle jelly beans, ride reindeer, and wear wigs, in a repertoire of acts limited only by the alliterative possibilities.

Sendak's alliterative stratagem highlights his sensitivity to the sound of his words. He arranges the alliterative phrases in parallel form for *Alligators'* narrative. The reptiles are busy "getting giggles" and "having headaches." The alliteration here previews its coming appearance in *Wild Things,* in which Sendak has the wild things "[roar] their terrible roars and [gnash] their terrible teeth."

Conclusion

Sendak's first two illustrated narratives (*Kenny's Window* and *Very Far Away*) are considered his worst. *Very Far Away* especially exhibits one of the worst-possible scenarios in a children's illustrated book—that the pictures simply reiterate what the words say. Nevertheless, together these books perform the necessary duty of providing starting points for Sendak's later successes.

The Nutshell Library, on the other hand, claimed a victory for Sendak. Not only did it say what Sendak wanted to say, but it said it in the way he wanted to say it. The words and pictures actively refer back and forth to one another in playful puns. The physical makeup of the book is a bibliophile's delight; its dimensions make it a curiosity to explore and a pleasure to peruse. Moreover, its physical traits are not trivial; they refer to the puns on the slipcase and inside the volumes.

With *Nutshell* Sendak began writing for an audience comprising both adults and children. The sophisticated puns of Johnny's "still life" on the table and of "lionizing" the king of beasts appeal to an older audience, whereas the antics of the alligators and *Chicken Soup*'s ditties appeal to any age. Five years later, Sendak came out with *Higglety Pigglety Pop!,* an illustrated book impossible to classify as being exclusively for either children or adults. Sendak was on his way to becoming an artist with a reputation for debunking the prescribed limits on "children's books."

4

Emblems in *Higglety Pigglety Pop!*

In *Higglety Pigglety Pop! or There Must Be More to Life* (1967) the main character, Jennie, is a dog with an insatiable appetite. She eats houseplants, tuna-on-rye, a half-dozen brown eggs, and even what she loathes—vanilla pudding. Facetiously, Sendak surrounds her with characters who wear costumes named after food: Rhoda wears leg-of-mutton sleeves, Mother Goose wears a muffin cap, and the pig wears a sandwich board complete with a front pocket of sandwiches (*Higglety Pigglety Pop!*, 6). As these visual puns bring to light, Sendak's illustrating style for *Higglety Pigglety Pop!* follows a nineteenth-century tradition. The nineteenth-century illustrating style more often noted in Sendak's work is his use of pen-and-ink with cross-hatching. (This is the same medium, though not the same line, George Cruikshank used for his illustrations of the fairy tales by the Brothers Grimm.) Unexamined thus far is Sendak's use, as well, of that nineteenth-century illustrating tradition which works hand in hand with the verbal narrative art of *Higglety Pigglety Pop!*—the iconographic tradition of illustrating with emblems.

An Emblematic Approach

To work in a Victorian iconographic tradition means that Sendak illustrates from an allegorical orientation. Such an approach demands three understandings between Sendak and his viewers: the use of emblems, their necessity for outside correspondences, and the approach's propensity for satire. Like his nineteenth-century mentors, Sendak follows in the footsteps of the eighteenth-century, pictorial-narrative illustrator William Hogarth in using details and allusions emblematically. An emblem by definition must collaborate with words to convey its meaning. It is not, then, a single image, such as an isolated picture of a tree; rather, it is a complex mixture of visual and verbal clues working together to express a synthesis of meaning. As Ronald Paulson puts it, "Words are to sentences as simple images are to complex images, or emblems."[1]

Given that Sendak uses emblems, he has to work with a mutual text, or shared beliefs, between his readers and himself. The working assumption in iconography is that the artist and audience understand the corresponding context for the picture. That context might be historical, mythical, political, or, of course, the text itself. In *Higglety Pigglety Pop!* the pictures interpret the story's text literally and figuratively; in the latter case, the pictures at times depict a metaphor implied by the text, though not stated directly.

Precedent of Phiz

Victorian illustrators built on the satiric tradition of Hogarth, often using their illustrative narrative as ironic commentary for the text. Such was the case with Harold Knight ("Phiz") Browne's illustrations for Charles Dickens's *Bleak House,* the intricate detective story satirizing the unjust handling of a case in Chancery and how it affected and interconnected persons from the lowest to the highest sectors of society. To highlight ironies in Dickens's narrative, Browne used emblematic details. For example, in chapter 39 Dickens makes quite apparent the ironic contrast between the attested earnestness of the lawyer, Mr. Vholes, and his actual fraudulence. He describes Vholes's office in Symond's Inn as "a large dust-bin."[2] In his accompanying illustration entitled "Attorney and Client, Fortitude and Impatience," Browne heightens the irony by adding emblem after emblem to the described "dust-bin" of an office.[3] Cobwebs in the corner, cobwebs on the clock, and a butterfly net all connote the trap of Vholes's inefficiency ensnaring Richard, the poor, unsettled young man whose one lasting commitment is to resolve the court case. Dickens mentions the cat in the corner waiting for a mouse that never comes, but he does not mention the figurine of Aesop's fox, which Browne places on the mantle, crouching for the grapes endlessly out of its reach. And while Dickens records the vapid promises of Vholes to devote his holiday "to making arrangements for moving heaven and earth" (Dickens, 553), he does not mention the empty bellows that Browne pictures resting behind Vholes's chair. Thus, Browne's emblematic details guide the reader to make the same sarcastic judgment of Vholes that Dickens suggests in his narrative.

Interpreting the Narrative Allegory

That Sendak should use an allegorical approach to compose his pictures for *Higglety Pigglety Pop!* makes sense, since he obviously composed his text from one: Jennie's physical insatiability parallels her spiritual discontent. The story opens with Jennie's surveying her comfortable life and wondering why she is still not happy. She then commences on a search for "something more," an element that soon materializes as an ambition to become the leading lady of the World Mother Goose Theatre, the one prerequisite being that she have experience. Jennie seeks the most immediate experience at hand—serving as a baby's nurse. Unfortunately, just as she assumes full responsibility for the child, a lion whisks it away. Out of a job and alone, Jennie despairs that having once had everything, she now has nothing. Miraculously, however, the baby reappears before her eyes as Mother Goose, informing her that now she does have experience. The very lion who stole the baby transports Jennie, along with the pig, cat, and Rhoda, to the "Castle Yonder," where the theater is located. Sendak ends the book with a pictorial cartoon, sans words, featuring Jennie as the leading lady in the play *Higglety Pigglety Pop!*

In her article describing students' interpretations of *Higglety Pigglety Pop!*, Mary-Agnes Taylor broadly divides the allegorical interpretations of the story into two camps: "those which interpret the story in a context of life—Jennie matures and becomes a successful actress; or, those which interpret it in a context of death—Jennie dies and goes to heaven."[4] Her students have based their interpretations on the story's traditional allusions and folkloric motifs, such as the journey and the forest; on its fairy-tale paradigms, for example, the rite-of-passage plot; and on concepts from Christian fundamentalism, interpreting the Castle Yonder as heaven (Taylor 1987, 143).

One of *Higglety Pigglety Pop!*'s most influential interpretations for it as an allegory about death and an afterlife is Selma Lanes's commentary in her biography of Sendak (150–71). As noted in chapter 1, Sendak had a sealyham terrier named Jennie, who died and he dedicated *Higglety Pigglety Pop!* to her. Accordingly, Lanes describes the whole book as "thinly disguised bits of autobiography" (160). In this way she is able to explain the book's most inscrutable details. As a case in point, Lanes notes that the parents' troubling abandonment of their child in *Higglety Pigglety Pop!* can be understood as a reference to Sendak's anticipation of his own parents' imminent deaths (160).

Such autobiographical insights serve as the basis for a fascinating psychoanalytic approach to *Higglety Pigglety Pop!* by Robert Kloss.[5] Noting Sendak's experiences with the death of his mother, the death of his pet, and his own near-death that surrounded the writing of *Higglety Pigglety Pop!*, Kloss reads the story as rooted in Freud's theory of a child's fear of abandonment (Kloss, 575). Freud believed this fear originates from an infant's inability to satisfy her or his own hunger (576). In this light, Kloss clarifies the interlocking meanings of the enigmatic metamorphosis of Baby into Mother Goose with the following explanation: "Baby's transformation into Mother Goose and Jennie's joining her acting troupe conflate Sendak, his mother, Jennie, and Baby into one central symbol with eating anxiety as the common bond" (576). In this way Kloss's approach offers Freud's theories as yet another plausible text for deciphering the enigmatic details of *Higglety Pigglety Pop!*

The Illustrations

Sendak uses his frontispiece to foreshadow emblematically the dominant tensions in Jennie's story. The accompanying text that informs this picture is the title itself on the facing page: *Higglety Pigglety Pop! or There Must Be More to Life.* In this picture Sendak centers Jennie in the middle of three emblematic clusters. His composition thus places Jennie metaphorically at a crossroads between life choices. Behind Jennie to her left hangs the *Mona Lisa,* the famous face contrasting with the unknown "mug" of Jennie. As an emblem, the meaning of *Mona Lisa* may be inscrutable. Yet, as art historian Patricia Crown notes, "The background of the real *Mona Lisa* is a dream landscape, fantastic and dark, which approximates Sendak's illustration on pages fifty and fifty-one."[6] These are the pages for the book's double spread that provides a visual transition from the ash wood to the magical stage. With this parallel, *Mona Lisa's* modeling her eternally blissful smile against her own fantastic backdrop may well allude to Jennie's performing her own eternally blissful act on the stage in Castle Yonder.

Sendak positions a window behind Jennie to her right. Windows and doors play a major role in the emblematic imagery throughout Sendak's illustrations as signs for opportunities. This one is uncharacteristically closed. Every other window and door in the book stands open, because in all other scenes, Jennie faces a promising opportunity. In the context of her comfortable life, Jennie ironically finds opportunities for happiness missing. Sendak shows Jennie facing what has been her life—she faces the vials and bowls that have brought her comfort and satisfied her palate. Here Sendak pictures these dishes emblematically empty, for Jennie finds her own life hollow.

In the next illustration (2), Sendak pictures Jennie's beginning a new direction in life. She has moved from being seated at the table, the place for gratifying her appetite, to being seated on the stairs, a place for moving and getting somewhere. She now faces out an opened window. Metaphorically, she looks "to open a new window," to face a new opportunity, as Auntie Mame recommends in *Charlie's Aunt.*

As an emblem, the plant pictured on the sill incarnates Jennie's spiritual condition. In the first picture, it is in full bloom, just as Jennie seems to be in her prime. It tells Jennie, "You have everything" (3). Specifically, she has two pillows, two kinds of pills, two kinds of drops, two bowls, two windows, one comb, one brush, one thermometer, and even "a red wool sweater" (3). In the next picture (4), not only is Jennie taking her leave, but she has taken all the leaves off the plant. With its stark image of stems in a pot, the plant now mirrors the nothingness Jennie is already beginning to encounter in her own life.

The interplay between Sendak's verbal narrative and his visual one continues in ironic comedy. Sendak writes that Jennie "packed everything in a black leather bag" (3). With "everything in the bag," so to speak, Jennie seems assured of a successful outcome, as the potted plant points out to her. It is the way Sendak pictures Jennie's leaving that comments on the meaning of the story: he pictures her departing with the bag in her mouth, thus making a visual pun on the implied colloquial expression that she is left "holding the bag." The illustration plays on this expression in two ways. First, Jennie is "left holding the bag" because she is to blame for decapitating the plant. Second, Jennie leaves "holding the bag" as a metaphor for her taking complete responsibility for her own happiness. She responds existentially to her desire for something more; to make her life meaningful, she acts—now by launching a quest and later by acting on stage.

In the ensuing pictures Sendak illustrates the bag next to Jennie as if it were her shadow. It is almost as large as she. Holding all the provisions she deems necessary for comfort in life, the bag encumbers her on her journey. As an emblem, the big black suitcase represents the abstract notion of Jennie's psychological baggage—her selfishness, her acquiring attitude for finding happiness—that impedes her on her quest.

In chapter 5 Jennie finally meets Baby. She also finally meets her match in terms of a "dogged," stubborn, willful attitude. Through his composition, Sendak cleverly depicts the parallel between the two characters by placing Baby on the floor, where a dog usually sits, and Jennie at the table, in Baby's chair (22). The whole chapter pokes fun at Jennie's acting like a baby and Baby's acting like a dog. As a veritable "dog in the manger," Baby prevents Jennie from enjoying the food she herself has no use for by biting Jennie's tail (24). Sendak describes the aftermath as a dog-eat-dog battle of the wills, writing "They sat staring at each other, growling and showing their teeth" (24). Things do indeed develop into a dogfight as "Baby [rolls] over Jennie" (26). Jennie, on the other hand, acts like a baby by egocentrically nursing her own needs. She selfishly eats all the child's food, even when Baby shows an interest in the pudding. When she calls Baby's parents, a primary motivation is to save her own hide. "What about me?" she moans into the telephone (29).

In chapter 6 Sendak again pictures Jennie "left [or leaving] holding the bag" (30)–only this time she assumes full responsibility for Baby's welfare. As she tells Rhoda, "I am personally taking Baby to Castle Yonder myself" (31). For this "backstair" operation, Sendak illustrates Jennie descending dark, winding steps (30).

It is at the bottom of the steps that Jennie finds the experience she seeks. Here Jennie faces the lion. Four times her size, he is neither docile nor friendly, as the lion in *Pierre* is; this lion has intimidating jowls and sharp teeth (34). In the verbal narrative Sendak builds suspense by metaphorically pushing Jennie up against a wall. She cannot guess Baby's name; neither will the lion be appeased by any of her possessions. Finally, writes Sendak, "There was only one thing left to do. Jennie sighed and stuck her head into the lion's mouth" (36). Here Jennie sacrifices herself for Baby. Surprisingly, Sendak chooses not to illustrate this turning point in the story.

Sendak instead includes the seemingly insignificant detail of an open door. In the verbal narrative he refers to this door at the beginning of the lion scenario with the lines "The staircase had come to an end at a wooden door. It creaked open and the lion roared, 'Another nurse, and a fat one too!'" (32). Here the text emphasizes Jennie's near-demise, which does indeed seem to be her "dead end." Yet the open door, as a very important emblem in the illustration, suggests the opposite: it connotes that this scene is not Jennie's end but an opportunity for a new beginning. In facing the lion's mouth, Jennie finally faces her unhindered opportunity for happiness.

Chapter 7 complements chapter 1 as its antithesis. It contrasts Jennie's alleged low point in the plot with her beginning high point. In chapter 1 Jennie has everything; in chapter 7, nothing. In chapter 1 Sendak pictures her larger than the potted plant and responsible for its defoliation; in chapter 7 the ash tree dwarfs Jennie and covers her with its leaves in an emblematic death scene (38, 41). The ash tree here serves as a classical emblem for death, making a visual pun on "ash" as a symbol for mortality: in the Jewish scriptures, Abraham defines his mortality before God with this symbol, saying, "I am but dust and ashes" (Gen. 18:27).

That Sendak should choose plants to serve as Jennie's interrogators in her metaphysical debates emblematically pits her against Nature. She begins her quest for life with seemingly full control over everything—except, of course, her appetite. By consuming the plant on the sill, Jennie illustrates her power over Nature. The houseplant itself is confined, whereas Jennie can move and travel. It sits at the mercy of Jennie's whims and appetite. In chapter 7 Sendak illustrates the power of Nature over Jennie. Looming above her, the ash tree towers over the runt in Sendak's composition. Now Jennie seems to be at the mercy of forces outside herself. Sendak draws the forest in naturalistic detail of tangled brambles and dense brush. Although Jennie is still free to move, Sendak hems her figure in between branches and the trunk of the wild ash (38). Two pages later it is as if Jennie were physically dead, for Sendak pictures her buried in ash leaves. He portrays her as powerless. Chapter 7 ends with the heroine "dog-tired," exhausted by her own failure.

In chapter 8 the interplay between the verbal narrative and the emblems in the illustrations reverberates with visual puns. Sendak pictures the full moon just above the horizon and Jennie facing it (42). As Jennie sits riveted toward the moon, she appears "moonstruck," or dazed. Sendak writes the accompanying narrative in a surrealistic style to evoke her trancelike state of mind: "Lions chased through Jennie's head. She caught one and was just about to bite when voices softly called: 'Jennie'" (43). From the age-old notion that moonlight causes insanity, the moon works here as an emblem to suggest Jennie's new irrational understanding that in having lost "everything," she has actually gained it.

In Jennie's epiphany, Baby reveals herself as the "moon-faced" Mother Goose to help Jennie make sense of her journey's nonsense. Sendak's metamorphosis of Baby into first the moon and then Mother Goose is a stroke of genius in terms of visual puns. As a colloquial expression, "moonlight" refers to holding down more than one job at once and thus plays on the notion of Mother Goose's part-time tasks of being Baby and the moon. "Moonshine" is also a term for "nonsensical talk," which is Mother Goose's specialty; she supposedly writes the silly script for *Higglety Pigglety Pop!,* which is actually Sendak's mimicking of the original "Hickory, Dickory Dock" (Taylor 1987, 143).

It is this queen of nonsense posing as the moon who "enlightens" Jennie on the meaning of her chaotic, or "higgledy piggledy," escapades. She fulfills Jennie's quest for "something more" by offering her something else—a leading role in a play. She explains that she has "chosen a very special play" for Jennie, "one to suit [Jennie's] very particular appetite" (48). This play is, of course, *Higglety Pigglety Pop!,* the stuff of supreme nonsense. It is Mother Goose who wisely guides Jennie to channel her destructive appetite into a creative act. That Sendak should put the answer Jennie is searching for into the mouth of Mother Goose promotes the original's campaign that wisdom can be found in her rhymes. In her introduction to the 1833 edition of *The Only True*

Mother Goose Melodies, an earlier "Ma'am Goose" scoffs at other "grannies" who say her verses "ought be laid aside for more learned books." Of these old women Mother Goose says, "Fudge! I tell you that all their batterings can't deface my beauties, nor their wise pratings equal my wiser prattlings."[7] All politics of original Mother Goose rhymes aside, the pictorial rhetoric of Sendak implies that here his fancy expresses a truth about Jennie's life.

The emblem of moonshine visually expresses an explanation for the kind of happiness Jennie has found. Inserting a double-spread picture between chapters 8 and 9, Sendak draws a shadowy landscape of forest, river, mountains, and moonshine. The death imagery of the ash tree is there. The life imagery of the water is there. But the moonshine transcends this life-and-death imagery of mere existence with multiple meanings of fantasy, nonsense, drama—things usually deemed unnecessary, yet pleasurable, in life. In contrast to the natural images, Sendak places Jennie's old black bag in the forest. Figuratively, the empty bag symbolizes Jennie's former unfulfilled life; now she leaves that behind her. In the context of the whole book, Jennie seems to be at the brink of a happiness founded on living creatively and sharing her creative art with others.

In chapter 9 Sendak stages the play *Higglety Pigglety Pop!* After only a half-page of text and one page showing the program, Sendak uses pictures, albeit with help from sparse bubble lines, to tell the story. The interplay of these few words and the full pictures makes an emblematic interpretation almost unavoidable.

Sendak literally enacts the visual pun of the title. The phrase "higgledy-piggledy," an adverb, means "in confusion." Likewise, the whole play works in a topsy-turvy fashion. Characters enter from the wings and exit out the window without a logical sequence. In the style of slapstick, the pig, posing as "Doctor Schwein," pours pills into Jennie's mouth before he jumps out the window; Jennie conks the lion on the head with a salami mop before he leaps through the window. Sendak ends the chaos with another pun: for the curtain call, the pig holds a signboard reading THE END, while the cat holds the end of the lion's tail. Sendak shows the audience the end of his tale here, but not the end of Jennie.

Simply because Jennie has found happiness does not necessarily mean she has completed her journey; the play is still left to be performed "every day and twice on Saturday" (69). Here the stage itself works as an emblem. Literally, the stage is a platform for the drama. Metaphorically, the "stage" can refer to Jennie's acting profession. In terms of the whole story, it is extremely significant that "stage" also means "a resting place on a journey." Jennie is thus on a stage and possibly in one—she may be in a phase of her development. Accordingly, Sendak keeps the window on stage fully open throughout the performance. He never bars the opportunity for change.

With respect, then, to the emblematic meaning of Castle Yonder, it can still be interpreted as a continuation of Jennie's earthly life or as a picture of her afterlife. Because Sendak visualizes it as a stage, it may not necessarily be a literal paradise, for that would make it a fixed, unchanging state for Jennie. Admittedly, Jennie tells her master that she has gone "away forever" (69); however, this statement could simply mean that she can never return to where she began. In Taylor's catalog of student responses to the story, she notes that if Castle Yonder is not locked into a one-to-one symbolism with heaven, it can have a variety of significances for Jennie—"maturity, personal achievement, fulfilled ambition, everyone's happy-ever-after, one's ultimate goal, dream come true, never-never land, the greener grass, reaching the unreachable, and Jennie's new everything that she has earned through sacrifice rather than received by gift" (Taylor 1987, 143). On the other hand, based on emblematic clues Castle Yonder may very well depict an otherworldly realm. Notably, Sendak draws the stage in a style different from that of the preceding illustrations. As Crown notes, "The stage scenes are simplified and abstracted compared with the earlier ones. It [the stage] is a different, shallower, less shadowed world" (Crown, 1990).

Sendak's illustration for the epilogue could be used to endorse

Castle Yonder as an emblem either for Jennie's heaven on earth or for her ultimate paradise. In the epilogue the narrative says that "Jennie is a star" (69). In fact, it says that Jennie "is the finest leading lady The World Mother Goose Theater ever had" (69). Transformed from an unknown face to a "very famous" actress (69), Jennie seems to have achieved a type of theatrical apotheosis. In the accompanying illustration Sendak implies as much by placing Jennie's bust in a circle reminiscent of the MGM lion logo. As an emblem, the circle surrounding Jennie connotes that she has "come full circle" in finding happiness. She started with having everything in chapter 1, moved to having nothing in chapter 7, and then ended having everything it takes to make her happy in chapter 9. Yet even Jennie cannot specify the exact nature of Castle Yonder. She says as much to her former master when she writes, "I can't tell you how to get to the Castle Yonder" (69).

Still, that Jennie fulfills her desires through the arts seems meaningful within the context of the book. Sendak tendentiously presents this foolish fantasy of Mother Goose as the cap and bells that indirectly speak the truth. After all, in a ruthless world it would be silly for Jennie to take risks for someone else. Yet the silliness of the rhyme, the confusion of the action and the irrationality of the plot compose the very structure that gives purpose, meaning, and delight to Jennie.

In this light Jennie's experience parallels the reader's if she or he also delights in such nonsense. Hans-Georg Gadamer, literary theoretician and phenomenologist, describes the aesthetic experience in general as if it were a quest. Richard Palmer paraphrases Gadamer's notion of an aesthetic search in the following way: "When we see a great work of art and enter its world, we do not leave home so much as 'come home.' We say at once: truly it is so! The artist has said what *is*. The artist . . . has not conjured up an enchanted never-never-land but rather this very world of experience and self-understanding in which we live, move, and have our being."[8] Such a subjective approach to Sendak's enigmatic *Higglety Pigglety Pop!* is helpful for understanding it. Because Sendak gives shape and form to this fairy tale through emblematic illustrations and text, he encourages vigorous audience participation in the reading experience. It is no superfluous detail, then, that at the moment of Jennie's epiphany, as she gazes into the full moon, Sendak draws her with her back to the audience (43). Such a composition necessitates that the viewer either sit beside Jennie or look over her shoulder to face the moonshadows with her.

Conclusion

What might be the approximate age of that viewer or reader is one of the most salient questions about *Higglety Pigglety Pop!* Undoubtedly, the answer is that the viewer could be any age from 8 to 80. In his verbal art Sendak alludes to the Mother Goose rhyme "Hickory, Dickory Dock," as well as to the existential principles of Kierkegaard. In line with Kierkegaard's paradigm, Jennie moves from being a "spectator" looking out her window to being an "actress" gainfully employed. She sequentially models the first two stages in Kierkegaard's theory: (a) his "aesthetic stage," when she initially focuses on gratifying her sensuous nature, and (b) his "ethical stage," when she morally offers her own life for Baby's.[9] In turn, Sendak's graphic art expects pictorial literacy from his adult viewers to recognize the dreamscape in da Vinci's *Mona Lisa* and the emblem of the ash tree, while it also encourages the intuitive expertise of its younger audience to interpret the surreal landscapes of moon and shadow as emblems of the fantastic. The richness of Sendak's work here unreservedly expresses that he is interested not in patronizing a primary audience but in offering the most engaging book he can to an audience uncategorized by age. This attitude of Sendak's goes hand in hand with his iconoclastic philosophy that books should not be censored for children but should instead be very, very good art for anyone—a philosophy that was scandalously realized in Sendak's picture-book trilogy.

5

The Picture Books' Fantasy Worlds: Architectural Solutions

Once lovingly dubbed the "Marie Curie of hopscotch and skip rope,"[1] Iona Opie, with her husband, Peter, pioneered in a new anthropological territory by watching children at playgrounds. In her observations Iona witnessed children successfully using "architectural solutions" to manage the problem of bullies. She noticed that the pestered children spared themselves from the troublemakers by seeking "a place apart, a kind of refuge" ("Playground," 30). "I'm sure I sound a bit simple," says Iona, "but it's my experience that big questions about good and evil sometimes come down to the question Have you anywhere else to go?" ("Playground," 30).

When faced with their own destructive impulses, the principal characters in Sendak's picture books must ask themselves the same question: Do I have anywhere else to go? They answer yes, escaping to havens that they themselves dream up. Each title of Sendak's three picture books bears the name of the imagined sanctuary: *Where the Wild Things Are* (1964), *In the Night Kitchen* (1970), and *Outside Over There* (1981). And most significant for the onlookers reading about these retreats is that Sendak makes the imaginary lands accessible to them too, through stylistic elements in his narrative. By using these stylistic elements, called "deictics" and "determinants," Sendak draws his readers into the safe fantasy worlds of Max, Mickey, and Ida.

The word "diectic" comes from the Greek root "deiktos," meaning "able to show directly"; thus, the Sendakian narrator uses deictics for joining the reader's point of reference to his or her own.[2] Sendak uses deictics to orient the reader to location and time in the fictive worlds of the picture books. He uses deictic words like "here" and "there," denoting space, and those like "then" and "now," denoting time; consequently, these spatial and temporal references encourage the reader to assume the same location and time frame as the narrator's if he or she is fully to understand the story (Traugott and Pratt, 275). For instance, should a narrator say "Now is the moment of truth" and the reader identify the "now" of his or her own circumstance as the moment of truth, he or she would not empathize with the speaker's situation. The "now" has to be the moment the princess who slept on the pea all night arrives, either well rested or with dark circles under her royal blue eyes, to greet the queen and hopeful prince.

Sendak sometimes moves the reader to share the narrator's perspective of the story by using definite articles and demonstratives. In addition, the definitive "the," "this," or "that," as opposed to the indefinite "a" or "any," prompts the reader to elaborate with his or her own details.[3] Sendak emphasizes this shared perspective by avoiding much description or detail. When the narrator introduces the setting of *Where the Wild Things Are* with the phrase "The night Max wore his wolf suit," the reader must at once assume she or he knows exactly the night spoken of. Emphasizing the shared perspective, the narrator uses another demonstrative in the second sentence with "That same night." Because the narrator does not elaborate in the beginning with such details as "The Saturday before Max's seventh birthday" or "On 22 November," the reader is free to imagine she or he knows exactly which night "the" night and later "that" night refer to.

Where the Wild Things Are

For *Wild Things,* Sendak designs a clear-cut plot with a definite beginning, middle, and end. In the beginning, Max acts like a "wild thing" and threatens to eat his mother, and so she confines him to his room without any supper. Max's room proceeds to change into a jungle and ocean. Max sails away in his own sailboat to the shore of some truly wild things. When they act unruly, Max reprimands them. For his revered control, the wild things crown Max king. He at once orders commencement of a glorious "rumpus," which Sendak pictures in the middle of the book for three double spreads without words. Afterward in the quiet, Max feels homesick. In the end, he decides to leave the wild things and return home, retracing his way in the boat. Back in his bedroom, he finds a toasty dinner waiting for him.

From the beginning of *Wild Things,* the narrator encourages the reader to share the fictive world of the book through Max's perspective. In the opening sentence the narrator first orients the reader to Max's circumstance. Like a good journalist, he sets the scene for the reader, first reporting the "person, place, and time" (Traugott and Pratt, 288): Max is the main character; he is at home; and he misbehaves at nighttime (Bagnall, 1980). As Elizabeth Closs Traugott and Mary Louise Pratt write in *Linguistics for Students of Literature,* "These [journalistic] orientations obviously serve to establish a shared universe with the reader" (288). Then too, by using very little detail—such as describing the mischief of Max as "one kind and another"—Sendak may be suggesting that the details are unimportant, but he also allows the reader to piece together those details from the clues in the pictures: a strangled teddy bear, a hammer held high, and a nervous terrier being chased by Max.

The narrator imposes the fictive time frame of the book on the reader by using the determinant "the" when he says, "The night." As in other tales of fancy, the story might have begun, "Once upon a time Max wore his wolf suit." But Traugott and Pratt point out that a once-upon-a-time beginning "presupposes the least shared knowledge and therefore requires the least work on the part of the reader" (288). Whereas the indefinite article "a" does not induce the reader to imagine anything, by beginning with "The night" the narrator assumes the reader imagines exactly the night spoken of. Consequently, the narrator invites the reader from the opening sentence to use his or her own imagination in entering the fictive world.

As the fantasy begins in the second sentence, the narrator establishes the reader's perspective in Max's perspective through references to location and time, references that expand the world of Max spatially and temporarily. The first place given is "Max's room," the square place confining Max. As the fantasy begins, Max's room expands into a forest; Max's ceiling expands into vines; and Max's walls expand into "the world all around," without corners or boundaries. Likewise, the time frame extends from "that very night" to "night and day" and then to "weeks" and further to "almost over a year."

Why would the narrator guide the reader into the fantasy world by expanding her or his sense of space and time? Because the narrator's directions to the reader parallel Max's experience as he fantasizes. That is, Max, in fantasizing, imagines himself out of his boxed-in bedroom and projects himself into another place and time. This psychological projection of self into a different place and time is the essence of fantasy. In telling the fantasy this way, the narrator presents Max as Max must be picturing himself, moving far away from his closed room to an exotic jungle. The narrator presents Max's journey to where the wild things are as if Max is rapidly moving through time. Using spatial prepositions—"through," "in," "out," and "over"—in reference to measurements of time, the narrator says Max sails

> through night and day
> and in and out of weeks
> and almost over a year.

With these prepositions the narrator enables the reader to watch Max as Max must imagine and, in a sense, watch himself sailing away.

When Max arrives at the place where the wild things are he is undaunted by their ferocity and calmly conquers them: "'And now,' [cries] Max, 'let the wild rumpus start!'" With the deictic "now" the narrator most fully merges the fantasy world of the reader with that of Max. After Max commands the rumpus, Sendak inserts three double-spread illustrations (six pages) of the wild things dancing, hanging from trees, and parading around. Like the effective pause of a live storyteller, the narrator's silence holds the reader's attention to the immediate moment. The story's "now" and the reader's "now" become one because the illustrations sans detailed description prompt the reader to imagine the narrative for the rumpus.

In direct contrast to the circumstance of the earlier command, when Max says "Now stop" he signals a return to restraint and control. Because Max uses the deictic "now" both to begin and to end the rumpus, the reader sees the warring attitudes inside Max: he wants to be both wild and in control "now" at the same time. In this way Sendak builds Max's fantasy to a logical climax. The rumpus marks the merging in time for Max's conflict both inside the fantasy and outside it.

The rumpus scene leaves Max unhappy with the wild things. He finds within himself the opposing strains of wildness and discipline. From this point, the narrator begins to guide the reader, with Max, back out of the fantastic land and toward a resolution in the ordinary world. As a foretaste of this resolution, the narrator presents Max daydreaming within the fantasy itself.

The narrator again expresses Max's daydream in terms of another time frame and another place. With the sentence "And Max the king of all wild things was lonely and wanted to be where someone loved him best of all," the narrator presents Max projecting himself into the future with the phrase "wanted to be" and imagining himself in another place with the phrase "where someone loved him best of all." As when Max initiated the fantasy, the narrator again expands the scope of the scene to distance Max from his immediate location. With the following sentence, "Then all around from far away across the world he smelled good things to eat," the narrator signals the expansion of space with the phrases "all around," "far away," and "across the world," and the reader, like Max, shifts her or his focus away from where the wild things are and back to Max's home even before Sendak has made the transition to home in the illustrations.

When Max decides to give up being king of the wild things and return home, the narrator guides the reader to retrace the journey. Just as the narrator earlier expanded Max's sense of time and place to construct the fantasy world, so too does he now contract the sense of time and place to reconstruct Max's ordinary world. Accordingly, the narrator presents the journey home in reverse order, saying,

> Max stepped into his private boat and
> waved good-bye
> and sailed back over a year
> and in and out of weeks
> and into the night of his very own room.

The narrator reorients the reader to the ordinary world by reminding the reader that Max is still the central character, that home is still the setting, and that the time of the action is still night.

Having guided the reader back into the ordinary world, the narrator must now guide him or her toward a resolution of the story. Here the narrator closes the story by saying that Max landed in his room, that he found his dinner prepared and waiting there, and that "it was still hot." Norma Bagnall points out that the detail of the hot supper waiting for Max at the end gives an emotional resolution to the story because it suggests feelings of love and security rather than those of anger and anxiety that Max felt in the beginning (Bagnall, 1980). But as a deictic reference to time, the hot supper firmly orients the location and time frame of Max in the ordinary world. The narrator's decision to end the story with the detail of Max's still-hot supper exposes the drastic difference between Max's time scheme in the fantasy world and that in the ordinary world. Through this detail the narrator suggests to the reader that although the fantasy took "almost a year" to get there and another year to get back, it has lasted but a moment.

In guiding the reader to find his or her way, along with Max, to and from the place where the wild things are, the narrator has been consistent; in short, he has presented the fantasy world of *Where the Wild Things Are* with clear-cut directions. Cornelia Meigs finds this orderliness vital for good fantasy. In the imaginary worlds, writes Meigs, "protagonists are often creatures of another world, the settings are over the border of reality, and time, as measured in our everyday lives, does not exist; yet the stories must be logical, event must follow in proper sequence, the plots must build up to a climax, and the outcome must be reasonable."[4] The narrator guides the reader into the fantasy through night, day, weeks, and a year, and then back out over a year, weeks, day, and into night. In strict monitoring, the deictics "now . . . start" and "Now stop!" limit the rumpus. Ironically, the fantasy world of where the wild beasts live has more predictable order and control than Max's ordinary world. In that latter world Max has no control over certain conditions. In the beginning, he cannot control his rowdiness, his anger, or his punishment; at the end, and in a different sense, Max could never have predicted being blessed by a hot supper. Thus, as a result of clear-cut directions into and out of the fantasy, Sendak creates a controllable place for Max to work out his confusion and, consequently, a non-threatening place where readers can explore their own encounters with wild things.

In the Night Kitchen

In Sendak's next picture book, *In the Night Kitchen*, the narrator again invites the reader to share in the fictive world of the book. That world is characterized by a Keystone Kop confusion and the sensuous, kinetic pleasures of rushing, soaring, swimming, sliding, and resting. At the book's beginning, noises awaken Mickey from bed. When he stands up to shout at the noisemakers, he falls far below into the "night kitchen." There he lands in a gigantic bowl of cake batter. Three fat cooks confuse Mickey for milk and proceed to mix him up. They are about to pop him into the oven when Mickey jumps out of the cake batter and into bread dough. He molds the dough into an airplane, which he then flies to the top of a towering milk bottle. Abandoning the plane, Mickey plunges headfirst into the milk and retrieves a pitcherful for the bakers below. With the cake-baking back under way, Mickey slides down the side of the milk bottle and this time lands in his own bed. More so than in *Wild Things,* the transitions from the ordinary world to the make-believe one and vice versa depend on the narrator's directions to the reader.

From the beginning of the story, the narrator directly appeals to the reader to share his perspective because it is from this vantage point that the perspective of the everyday world is established; in other words, the narrator relies on the reader's siding with him to form the status quo, creating the situation of the ordinary world existing outside the book and the make-believe world existing inside it. In the first sentence, the narrator directly addresses the reader as "you," placing the entire sentence in the form of a question: "Did you ever hear of Mickey . . . ?" The narrator's choice of "you" and his question establish the relationship between himself and reader to create the shared everyday world. This detail is necessary for the fantasy to work because, as the book opens, the dream has already begun. Mickey has already heard the "racket," as the words in the pictures denote "THUMP," "DUMP," "CLUMP," and "LUMP." By establishing the reasonable world safely in tandem between narrator and reader, the narrator offers a nonthreatening invitation into a dream world of surprise flights and splash landings.

In his opening invitation to the reader the narrator also gives clear, if fanciful, spatial directions for where the reader is to locate the dream world. Mickey falls "through the dark," "out of his clothes," past his parents, and into the kitchen. This scenario is, of course, impossible—if Mickey falls out of his bed, he will hit the floor; he cannot fall through floors, ceilings, walls, and basements.

This fanciful way of introducing the reader to the imaginary world Mickey is entering bears a striking resemblance to the way children initiate games. In her book *Nonsense* Susan Stewart explains how nonsense gestures in various forms establish the boundaries for children's games: "In children's games, the formation of a boundary is intrinsic to getting in or out of the game. The way to form such a boundary is to make a play gesture, a movement that sends the message 'this is play' and marks off the particular space and time that will characterize the game. This movement may take the shape of a mock attack or stunt, by beginning a fiction or by making a ludicrous expression."[5] Two points from Stewart's explanation are strikingly appropriate for the opening of *In the Night Kitchen*. First, in "beginning a fiction" by telling the reader something that absolutely could not happen, the narrator alerts the reader that "This is play" or "This is fantasy." The narrator's description of Mickey's impossible fall marks the boundary for a strange fantasy world with its own rules of what can and cannot happen. Second, the act of Mickey's falling through the dark characterizes the entire fantasy temporally and spatially. The fantasy takes place exclusively at night and includes repeated vertical movement. But this downward fall also metaphorically characterizes the location of the night kitchen. It is below Mickey. Metaphorically, the night kitchen's location below Mickey suggests the imaginative world below Mickey's consciousness, the subconscious realm where dreams take place.

In the second sentence the narrator reminds the reader that she or he is still a close companion with Mickey on this adventure by means of the reference to "we." The narrator slips the inclusive pronoun into his description of the action in the night kitchen:

> Where the bakers who bake till the
> dawn so we can have cake in the morn
> mixed Mickey in batter.

Granted, in English "we" may or may not include the specific listener; rhetorically, however, the narrator offers his listener the opportunity to pretend he or she eats cake in the morning.

As in *Where the Wild Things Are,* in *Night Kitchen* Sendak faces the same problem of signaling a sense of time—here, a sense of immediate, time—within the fantasy that is different from that in the ordinary world without. In *Wild Things* he expresses the difference in Max's subjective sense of time during the fantasy and his objective sense of time in the ordinary world by creating the contrast of the length of the voyage (more than two years) and the piping-hot supper waiting by Max's bed. In *Night Kitchen* Sendak reverses the sensation of time, making the dream sense of time seem very short, while the actual length of the dream in the ordinary world is lasting all night long.

At the focal point of the fantasy, the bakers plead for Mickey to get milk for the morning cake, and the narrator says Mickey flies up to retrieve the milk from the top of a giant milk bottle. The narrator's terse phrases "and up," "and up," and "and over the top" create a fast-paced rhythm to accompany Mickey's quick flight. The illustrations, as Joseph Schwarcz points out in *Ways of the Illustrator*, also make the flight seem speedy through Sendak's illustrative technique of "continuous narration," whereby Sendak breaks the action of Mickey's flight into four separate pictures across a double spread, similar to the depiction of action in a comic strip. Schwarcz feels that the splicing of this one action into "four frames serves to increase the sense of urgency in the viewer's mind" (Schwarcz, 29). Then too, as pointed out earlier in the discussion of Sendak's illustrations for Ruth Krauss's *A Very Special House,* the repetition of the figure of Mickey creates a sense of "fleeting action" (Schwarcz, 29).

Schwarcz notes that within each frame Sendak also draws the moon sinking on the horizon, suggesting that the flight lasts the length of the nighttime. "A contrast exists," Schwarcz says, "between Mickey's subjective sense of time and objective time" (30). This second notion is confirmed for the reader when at the end of the book, after Mickey has completed his mission, he heralds the dawn with a loud "COCK-A-DOODLE-DOO!" and then falls back into his bed, as the sun rises in the background.

Similar to his technique in *Wild Things,* the Sendakian narrator involves the reader as a participant within Mickey's fantasy not only by what he does say but also by what he does not say.

For two whole pages, the narrator keeps mum. While Mickey hovers in an airplane over the wide mouth of the looming milk bottle, the bakers wait below like pregnant women with their hands resting on their bellies. As the stars twinkle and the flags wave over the nightscape, the narrator remains silent. As in *Wild Things,* this panorama offers the reader the chance to fill the gap in the narrative with her or his own explanations and conjectures; the reader may choose to deliberate or to rush ahead with a quick page turn to the next action.

Similar still to the technique in *Wild Things* for ushering the young adventurer home is that at the end of Mickey's fantasy in the night kitchen the way home is given in reverse. Yet for Mickey, the locations for his ordinary world and his fantasy one seem to have switched places: whereas at the beginning of the dream Mickey falls down into the night kitchen, but at the end of the dream he falls down into his bed, or, as the narrator explains, Mickey "slid down the side / straight into bed / cakefree and dried." This change of direction means, spatially, that Mickey's fantasy world has switched places with his real world. Before, the fantasy world was beneath Mickey, a placement metaphorically suggesting Mickey's subconscious activities, those activities which conceptually exist beneath the surface of things. Because Mickey's bedroom now stands below the night kitchen, its new location also suggests a place for activity beneath the surface of things. This switch in location of everyday and dream worlds suggests that Mickey's two worlds have merged. The narrator thus slyly hints (as Mickey knowingly smiles) that the whole escapade in that checkered-linoleum kitchen actually took place in his bedroom, or, more precisely, inside Mickey's head. Poetically, Sendak summarizes this synthesizing reversal through the cartoon balloons for Mickey's speech: as the naked, dreaming boy falls into bed, he shouts, "OH!"; as the blanketed boy smiles from bed, he laughs, "HO!" The same word read forward and backward suggests an Alice-through-the-looking-glass key to the fantasy: like Alice, Mickey dreams the whole charade, subconsciously using images from his daily life in a pastiche of dream motifs.

The final clue the narrator gives the reader that the world of the night kitchen is a make-believe place consists of closely comparing it with a common realm in the ordinary world that often poses as real but is actually fantastic—the world of advertising. In his illustrations Sendak has set up this comparison all along, concocting the cityscape out of oversize bottles and boxes of pantry goods from soaps to cereals and then labeling those containers with slogans promising mercantile miracles, such as "Sweet At All Times," "Absolutely Pure," "Does the Trick," and "Best." And so in the farewell to the reader, when the narrator says, "And that's why, thanks to Mickey / We have cake every morning," he assumes the rhetoric of an advertiser using absolute language ("every morning") for a cause-and-effect situation. Using the inclusive "we" again heightens the narrator's ploy because as most young readers will readily realize, they seldom if ever have cake for breakfast.

The layout for this adieu complements the narrator's commercial tone, for Mickey is pictured as a logo in the middle of a geometric sun design, with the text encircling him like a label. In this way the narrator respects the reader's intellect by letting him or her in on the secret that the night kitchen is truly a fantasy, rather than flatly calling the extravaganza a lie.

In summary, from the narrator's direct address to the reader in the beginning with the question, "Did you ever hear of Mickey?" through his reference to the reader and himself in the middle with "we" until his ending use of "we," he seeks to share the fantasy world of Mickey with the reader. This shared perspective genuinely creates the boundaries of the everyday world. That acknowledged genuineness allows the reader a safe seat beside Mickey in his flight of fancy.

Outside Over There

In *Outside Over There* the narrator guides the reader, as the narrators do in the other two picture books, with deictics mapping out the location and time frame of the fantasy. Yet unlike the narrators' directions in *Wild Things* and *Night Kitchen,* the narrator's directions in *Outside Over There,* as well as the story's meaning, are sometimes elusive.

Because Ida's parents do not do so, Ida must watch her baby sister. But Ida instead grows inattentive and busies herself by playing her horn. Consequently, goblins kidnap the baby and leave a changeling in her place. When Ida discovers the impostor, she rushes to save her sister. But she makes a blunder: she commences the rescue mission backward. The narrator says, "She climbed backwards out her window into outside over there." Ida almost loses track of the goblins, until she hears a song from her father warning her to turn around. Once Ida reverses her direction, she finds the goblins immediately. Playing her horn, Ida hypnotizes them to dance uncontrollably. Similar to Sambo's tigers' melting into butter, Ida's goblins churn themselves into a stream. Ida then finds her sister and carries her home. There Ida encounters another warning from her father, this time via a letter in which he admonishes her to continue to look after the baby. It is a difficult ending for a difficult story.

Geraldine DeLuca argues that *Outside* presents a fantasy world inaccessible to children.[6] She claims the text is obscure because of its "allegorical sensibility," a characteristic she describes as having "layer upon layer of meaning" (DeLuca 1984, 4). Although the story does seem obscure in places, it is not altogether an inaccessible journey into fantasy for children to take if they make the journey from Ida's perspective, not their own. Ultimately, the obscurity of the narrator's attempts to share with the reader the fictive world of Ida's "outside over there" is appropriate, for the narrator's directions to the reader are open-ended to the degree that Ida's own sense of time and location is open-ended.

Through his clues to the reader, the narrator re-creates a sense of the difficulty of Ida's everyday world. As in *Night Kitchen,* when the reader turns the first page the fantasy is already in progress in the illustrations—goblins are lurking in the pictures' corners. Yet for the first three pages the narrator does not mention the hooded figures; he simply describes the "facts" of Ida's everyday world. True to the Sendakian picture book, the narrator shares the story's point of view with the reader by presenting the person, place, and time in the first sentence:

When Papa was away at sea,
and Mama in the arbor,
Ida played her wonder horn
to rock the baby still—
but never watched.

Here the narrator presents Ida as the main character. By inference, the reader discerns Ida's situation. She is not with her father, for he is at sea. She is not with her mother, for she is in the arbor. Therefore, Ida seems to be alone at home. In this way the narrator suggests that the motivating problem for Ida is her baby sister. With both parents preoccupied, Ida faces the tedium of looking after an infant alone.

Most atypical about this beginning for a Sendakian picture book is the way the narrator establishes a shared sense of time associated with Ida's problem. Ida's everyday time frame does not have the exactness of time expressed in the openings of the other two picture books; the action here is instead presented in duration. In the other books' openings, Max "wore" his wolf suit and Mickey "heard" the racket. Using the past tense, the narrators of those books express the actions as completed. But though the narrator in *Outside* gives Ida's own action as completed, saying she "played her wonder horn," he presents Papa's action as in duration. By using the deictic phrase "When Papa was away," the narrator leaves ambiguous the exact time of Ida's father's departure and return. Consequently, Ida may only have begun to take care of her sister, or she may have been baby-sitting her for a suspended length of time. The open-endedness in the narrator's clues re-creates for the reader the sense of pending time Ida must be feeling in charge of a baby.

In orienting the reader to Ida's world, what the narrator does not tell the reader is as important as what he does. As noted, the narrator does not tell the reader about the hooded figures. Assuming that the narrator recognizes these goblins as part of Ida's world, he never identifies the mysterious creatures; he simply refers to them in the second stanza with the definite article "the"— "So the goblins came," he says. This use of "the" shows that the narrator assumes the reader knows exactly those goblins to which he refers (Ong, 13). With both of these assumptions, then, the narrator guides the reader to enter imaginatively into Ida's world, a world that contains both the ordinary and the fantastic.

Thus far, in both narrative and illustrations Ida seems aloof from both her everyday world and her fantasy world. In her ordinary world, Ida ignores her sister; in her imaginary world, she ignores the goblins as they carry her sister away. Ida's indifference works appropriately with the sense of pending time established at the beginning of the story, for it epitomizes her feeling of boredom. The reader may also feel aloof because the narrator's directions so far have been extremely limited.

Ida's response to both worlds changes when her sense of time changes. The narrator points the reader to Ida's sense of immediacy in the story through a change in circumstances and through the deictic "now." Circumstances change for Ida when she realizes her baby sister has been stolen by goblins. The narrator signals her present-tense sense of urgency with the phrase "Now Ida in a hurry." It is the first time within the plot that Ida has acknowledged the goblins. When the narrator says "Ida mad knew goblins had been there," the narrator's "there" means "there with Ida."

The circumstances surrounding the present time for Ida are similar to those surrounding the present time for Max in *Where the Wild Things Are*. When Max says, "And now . . . let the wild rumpus start!" he suddenly changes his actions from calm to uproarious behavior. When he subsequently orders, "Now stop!" he suddenly changes from a wild to a tame boy. Likewise for Ida— when the narrator says "Now," Ida undergoes a drastic change of behavior, switching from neglecting her sister to aggressively seeking after her.

The narrator further points the reader to Ida's new sense of purpose by at once giving a generous helping of directions. He notes that Ida goes "backwards out her window into outside over there." Here the narrator gives six different directions: "back-

wards," "out," "into," "outside," "over," and "there." Just as it is
difficult for the reader to determine exactly which way Ida is
going, so too does Ida herself become disoriented, being described
as "foolish" and "whirling." The narrator thus describes the passage into the fantasy world of "outside over there" so that the
reader knows just as much as Ida.

When, however, Ida's sense of direction becomes so confused,
her father intervenes with just enough information to get her on
the right course. The deictics in Papa's song literally and figuratively mark the turning point for Ida. Literally Papa sings for Ida
to "turn around," and figuratively Ida does an about-face in her
behavior. Whereas earlier Ida's disobedience—her never watching the baby—led to the kidnapping, now her obedience leads to
the rescue.

When Ida obeys her papa, the narrator captures her acquired
sense of security by explaining to the reader that Ida is now in a
specific location. No longer is she spinning aimlessly without her
feet on the ground; she is, says the narrator, now "smack in the
middle of a wedding."

Once Ida finds herself centered in the wedding, the narrator
presents what she sees to the reader as Ida herself discovers it,
that these previously mysterious-looking goblins actually resemble her own younger sibling. As the narrator puts it, the goblins
appear to be "just babies like her sister!" Even though the narrator speaks in the third person, he establishes a shared
perspective between Ida and reader (Traugott and Pratt, 289).
Spiritually, Ida experiences a breakthrough. She has faced both
her sister and the goblins and seen both for what they are—a
veritable "hubbub," as she says. The narrator captures Ida's final
confrontation with her negative feelings toward her sister by cen-
tering her in an event that metaphorically mandates the union of
opposites: a marriage dance. Here Ida can face the truth, as the
reader does alongside her, that troublesome sprites (the goblins)
sometimes take the form of lovable babies (her sister).

With Ida's reconciling insight shared with the reader, the former sense of pending time is stopped. Here within the haven of
Ida's imaginary world, the narrator presents her with a sense of

progressive, fast-paced time. Now when Ida plays her wonder
horn for these goblin babies the narrator directs the reader to a
moving sense of time with the deictics "at first," "then," and
"until":

> The goblins, all against their will, danced slowly at first,
> then faster until they couldn't breathe.

Each of the deictic words signals a marking off of time in progress.

In the next sentence, referring to the goblins with the demonstrative "those," the narrator directs the reader to acknowledge
the same goblins that Ida does. In this way the narrator guides
the reader to discover with Ida the one "goblin" who does not
change into the stream:

> Except for one who lay cozy in an eggshell,
> crooning and clapping as a baby should.
> And that was Ida's sister.

With the deictic phrase "Except for one" and the deictic word
"that," the narrator guides the reader to view the scene from Ida's
perspective.

After her purging confrontation in the safety of her own fantasy
world, Ida redeems her sense of present time and immediate action in the everyday world. The narrator describes her journey
home, beginning in the present. "Now," he said, Ida starts for
home.

The narrator's use of deictics again points the reader to visualize the path as Ida sees it. The return journey home is as laby-
rinthine as that from home, but the directions are more specific.
The narrator directs the reader to "the stream that curled like a
path along the broad meadow and up the ringed-round hill to her
Mama." With such specificity, even though the way home is not
as straight as the crow flies, it is clearly cut, and Ida has the
energy to complete the journey while holding her baby sister.

That Ida's trek home is uphill has symbolic nuances different
from the emotional tones at the endings of *Wild Things* and *Night*

Kitchen. Max sails back "into the night of his very own room where he [finds] his supper waiting for him"; his journey is horizontal—not as difficult as Ida's upward climb. And Mickey returns home by simply falling into bed "cakefree and dried," the narrator's pun on "cakefree" for "carefree" serving to end Mickey's story with a lighthearted tone. But with Ida, her rising path and twisting trail home symbolize the difficulty of her experience, for when she gets there she finds not Papa but his letter waiting for her.

With Papa's letter the narrator again establishes the sense of pending time for Ida. The future tense in the phrase "I'll be home one day," coupled with the standing command that "little Ida must watch," projects resolution of Ida's predicament into the future. In her fantasy world Ida could aggressively take time into her own hands. The narrator said she gathered her cloak and horn "now," and when she exited the fantasy land, the narrator again marked her departure with the time of "now." Ida proved that she could control the present time, but she cannot control the future and make her father return sooner or more definitely.

The story ends in a remarkable way. The narrator closes with one line, as Ida's response to Papa's letter—"Which is just what Ida did," the "Which" referring to Ida's obediently watching "the baby and her Mama for her Papa." Because Ida cannot change her circumstances of waiting and watching, she changes herself. Ignoring her responsibility to watch her sister in the beginning, she now claims that charge. It is a wondrous conclusion to a story about fantasy because Ida matures in a reasonable, unmagical way.

In *Outside Over There* the delicate boundary between the ordinary and the fantastic worlds, the narrator's circuitous pathways to and from the fantasy, and the multiple levels of fantasy experienced by Ida make for a complicated narrative. The narrator's confusing description of the journey to the fantasy and his convoluted directions for the journey back home do at first seem inaccessible pathways to and from fantasy. Yet Wayne Booth, in *The Rhetoric of Fiction,* argues that before a reader criticizes or praises a piece of literature for its obscurity, he or she must consider the appropriateness of that obscurity for the particular work.[7] Here the possible discomfort in the reading experience parallels the difficulty of Ida's experience. She is the sole person responsible for her baby sister, since both parents are busy. The tedium of watching her sister contains mixed emotions of love, dislike, jealousy, and boredom. These are troubling sentiments to confess when one wants to please one's parents. Because the narrator gives Ida's dream adventure to the reader through at-times-confusing deictics but specifically from Ida's perspective, the reader's experience of reading *Outside Over There* may be as cathartic as Ida's own experience in the book.

Conclusion

Ironically, it was Sendak's picture-book trilogy—*Where the Wild Things Are, In the Night Kitchen,* and *Outside Over There*—that confirmed his skill with words. The artist, regarded primarily as an illustrator, emerged as a competent writer as well. At the Fifth Annual Conference of the Children's Literature Association, held at Harvard University in 1978, Sendak asserted his talents for both graphic and literary art as interdependent in the picture book. In an interview he explained, "I have been so often praised for the pictures in my picture books, as though in spite of the words, the pictures were good. And yet I know that I would not be an illustrator without words."[8] It was *Wild Things*, winner of the Caldecott Medal, that established Sendak as an outstanding narrative writer for children. From a New Critical perspective, the brief text of *Wild Things* is admirably tight, with a controlled conflict and resolution and with a symmetrical plot. Sendak shapes the fantasy with an Aristotelian beginning, middle, and end—first establishing the initial problem in the ordinary world, then launching its development into a fantasy world, and finally anchoring the resolution firmly back in Max's everyday setting.

Night Kitchen does not share *Wild Things*'s "narrative linear causality," and for this reason critics have ranked it second to *Wild Things*'s artfulness. Nevertheless, William Touponce argues—and I agree with him—that *Night Kitchen* equally offers the reader aesthetic pleasure by raising tactile and kinetic sensations through its "poetic word-images."[9] Sendak's word images of batter and dough present archetypes of an imaginative, malleable pâte that Mickey shapes and forms by his own control. It is the reader's ability to identify with these primordial images of creativity in *Night Kitchen,* argues Touponce, that makes it a supreme piece of illustrated literature.

It follows that *Outside* has not been as highly received as either *Wild Things* or *Night Kitchen.* Again, judged by its definition of conflict and resolution, *Outside* certainly does not offer a sense of surety in the beginning or complete peacefulness at the end. But judged on whether or not it shares with the reader the troublesomeness of Ida's experience, I believe it succeeds.

As a creator of fantasies, Sendak has shown us his versatility to design *Night Kitchen* in the personality of Grand Central Station and *Outside* in the tone of a Frankish castle on the Rhine. Refreshingly, he never follows the same blueprint, yet his blueprints always include directions for the reader on how to visualize his fantasy worlds. His ability to so artfully stage the settings of these separate fantasies makes him a master storyteller, for children read, writes Carolyn Horovitz, "for the living experience, the book and the child becoming one in a kind of osmosis [*sic*] state."[10] Such enjoyable transport from their immediate circumstances also vicariously affords young readers their own quiet place for escape.

6

The Picture Books' Syncopated Rhythm

The syncopated rhythm of the narrative is a prominent characteristic in all three Sendakian picture books. As Geraldine De-
Luca points out, the language constantly moves "in and out of
rhyme" and in and out of prose (DeLuca 1984, 4). Though this
capricious shifting from prose to verse would seem to create a
madcap confusion of meter, a second look shows that the shifts
actually create order. In each of his three picture books—*Where
the Wild Things Are, In the Night Kitchen,* and *Outside Over
There*—Sendak's shifts from the rhythm of prose to the rhythm
of verse control the stories' frightening or chaotic effect. When
the protagonists—Max, Mickey, and Ida—show command of the
situation or their feelings, Sendak writes in prose; when, however, they experience a confusing situation or emotion, Sendak
controls that bewilderment by writing in the regular rhythm of
verse.

The premise of Sendak's shifting from prose to verse for aesthetic control in his picture books resembles Wordsworth's theory
for controlling painful sentiment in his poetry. The older romanticist's rubric that "all good poetry is the spontaneous overflow of
powerful feelings" is often quoted apart from its context in his
"Preface to Lyrical Ballads."[1] This misquoting belies the fact that

Wordsworth also states in the "Preface" that the more powerful the feelings are, the more disciplined the language must be in its sound, especially in its rhythm, if it is to have the desired effect on its readers. In a less famous passage Wordsworth specifically states that the controlled rhythm of verse expresses painful sentiment better than the random rhythm of prose: "There can be little doubt but that more pathetic situations and sentiments, that is, those which have a greater proportion of pain connected with them, may be [better] endured in metrical composition, especially in rhyme, than in prose" (Wordsworth, 459). When painful emotions are expressed in meter, writes Wordsworth, the reader finds a compensating "pleasurable surprise from the metrical arrangement" (459). Known for his unflinching look at the agonies of childhood, Sendak chooses verse to express the uncomfortable confusions of childhood in an orderly manner.

To analyze this switch, I describe prose as having a random rhythm and verse as having a regular one. Prosodists, however, disagree on the way verse shows its regularity of rhythm. Laurence Perrine classifies verse as language with metrical stress, defining verse as "an arrangement of language in which the accents occur at apparently equal intervals in time."[2] For Karl Shapiro and Robert Beum, though, other features besides meter cause language to have regular rhythm. These authors say that when language shows "some quality of the syllables, such as stress or quantity . . . either strictly or at least relatively regularized," it is verse.[3] Sendak does not always write his narrative with accents occurring, as Perrine would say, at regular intervals; the rhythm is not always as metrical as ti-DUM, ti-DUM, ti-DUM. Yet at times Sendak does create a pattern of sound with syntax, alliteration, or syllables arranged so regularly that the rhythm is too predictable to be prose. As Shapiro and Beum would say, there is some regular "quality of the syllables," enough to judge such passages as verse. For this analysis, I use the term "prose" to describe passages with randomly occurring stress and the term "verse" to refer to highly patterned passages, whether patterned by stress or by a repeated quantity of syllables, as in syllabic verse.

Where the Wild Things Are

In *Wild Things* Max faces three uncomfortable experiences, all concerning wild, unruly behavior. In the opening scene he acts like a wild thing; in the central scene he encounters the wild actions of monsters; and in the penultimate scene the monsters imitate the wild action of Max. Yet the wilder the action, the more controlled the language becomes.

The opening discomfort for Max stems from his mother's punishing him for acting like a wild thing, a situation that creates feelings of anger and rebellion in young Max. Sendak puts aesthetic distance between the reader and Max's uncomfortable feelings by writing this opening scene in syllabic verse. Here Sendak arranges phrases or lines expressing similar ideas to have the same number of syllables (Bagnall, 1980). In the opening line, the verb phrases "wore his wolf suit / and made mischief" each express what Max did to be wild, and each contain four syllables. The next two phrases, "of one kind / and another," both allude to the mischief of Max and have three and four syllables, respectively. As if in compensation for the difference in exact syllable count, the phrases each show one dominant stress—"of ońe kind / and anóther"—and thus sound rhythmically balanced. In the next two lines, the first expresses directly and the second indirectly what Max is acting like, and both lines contain seven syllables apiece:

> his mother called him "WILD THING!"
> and Max said "I'LL EAT YOU UP!"

Max receives a dreadful punishment in the final line: he "[is] sent to bed without eating anything." Having a slight caesura between "bed" and "without," the line breaks into two phrases. With six syllables in the first phrase and seven in the second, the two phrases show three dominant stresses each: "šo Máx wǎs sént tŏ béd wǐthóut eátiňg ańythǐňg." Sendak expresses the emotional experience of Max's acting wildly, losing control, and getting punished in lines patterned by repeated quantities of syllables and stress. Though the narrative does not look like verse, the rhythmic balance in quantity of sound classifies this passage as syllabic verse.

Max's wildness is challenged only by that of the wild things themselves. When Max first encounters the wild things, they act ferociously. For this situation, Sendak repeats words, syntax, and sounds, creating a regular pattern of stress. He repeats the words "their terrible" for each action; he writes parallel syntax for each terrible action, having the wild things roar, gnash, roll, and show. Consequently, Sendak creates a cadence out of chaos: "thĕy roaŕed theĭr térrĭbĭe roárs aňd gnaśhed theĭr térrĭbĭe teéth / aňd rolled thĕir térrĭbĭe eyés aňd shówed thĕir térrĭbĭe cláws." Reinforcing the cadencelike quality of the language, he also repeats sounds. The passage bears heavy alliteration in consonants and consonant blends: "they," "their"; "terrible," "teeth"; "roared," "roars," "rolled"; "gnashed," "showed." Assonance also appears in "their terrible" and "rolled" and "showed." Through his legerdemain of prosody, Sendak turns what might have been leering monsters into laughable ones.

When, in the following episode, the action of the scene becomes controlled—that is, when the scene's action shifts from roaring wild things to a king's taking command—Sendak likewise shifts from metrical rhythm to prose. From the time Max takes charge and commands the wild things to "BE STILL!" the narrative rhythm is random. The verb phrases "BE STILL!," "tamed them," "they were frightened," and "they called . . . and made" alternate between the passive and active voice, in contrast to the previously parallel syntax for the uproar. Even the passage's appearance on the page, with its uneven line lengths, reinforces the random sound of the rhythm.

Later Sendak again juxtaposes two episodes of entirely different emotional tenor. In the first Max quietly regains control of his emotions; in the second, which immediately follows, he is threatened with being eaten alive by the wild things. For the episode describing Max's repentance, Sendak, although using some alliteration in "all around from far away across," writes in random rhythm. In contrast, he writes the threat of the wild things not

only in meter but also in rhyme. The end rhymes of "go," "so," and
"No" and the straight iambs in each line make a singsong farce
out of the threat. This doggerel verse so neutralizes the wildness
of the wild things that one wonders why some critics feared the
monsters would scare children, for the more fiercely the wild
things act, the more regular does Sendak make the stress and
rhyme.

The shifts in rhythm are not always as abrupt as in the afore-
mentioned passages. Sendak tailors his rhythmic shifts to suit
the degree of change in emotional intensity. Thus, when Max returns home from where the wild things are, the change in emotional intensity is gradual, and Sendak accordingly changes the
rhythm from verse to prose gradually. When the wild things sur-
round Max as he begins his journey home, Sendak, as before, composes their roaring and gnashing in cadencelike rhythm. As Max
makes his way home, the scene quiets. Accordingly, the rhythm
of the text relaxes from a regular cadence to what Selma Lanes
describes as the "lilt of free verse" (Lanes, 87), demonstrated by
the passage in which Max leaves the wild things

> and sailed back over a year
> and in and out of weeks
> and through a day
> and into the night of his very own room.

At this point, though the narrative does not say explicitly that
Max tames himself, the rhythm of the final line shows that he
does: the rhythm is straight prose. Sendak resolves the story with
this final line focused on Max's supper, described simply as "and
it was still hot." The brevity of the line makes it difficult to identify the rhythm strictly as either regular or random. But it is safe
to say that the two heavy stresses at the end ("still hot") prevent
a metrical iambic line. Further, because the line stands alone on
the page, it tends not to be read as a unit of rhythm with other
lines or phrases. In short, the end neither sounds nor looks like
verse; it is prose. This prose contrasts with the syllabic verse at
the beginning of the story, wherein Max felt angry and rebellious

for being sent to bed without supper. Now that Max realizes his mother loves him, he can return freely home as ex-king of the wild things—and, with Max's wildness tamed, Sendak can end the book in prose.

It has become a Sendak trademark for each pictured book to end with prose instead of verse. No matter how flamboyant the fantasies become in the middle of Sendak's picture books, the stories always end in prose or "prosaically." They end in the rhythm of the everyday world, and for Max that means giving up the wild world of the jungle for the orderly world of his bedroom. It also means giving up being king of the wild things in order to be a hungry boy who gets to eat a hot supper.

In the Night Kitchen

In *Night Kitchen* the protagonist, Mickey, also ventures to a "wild" place—but one that is chaotic, not filled with ferocious beasts. Three bustling bakers—each a double for a gargantuan Oliver Hardy—create the chaos. To begin with, they initiate a racket that awakens Mickey from his sleep. Then Mickey, falling into the bakers' batter, literally gets mixed up in the muddle. The bakers mistake him for milk, and this confusion remains throughout the fantasy. As in *Where the Wild Things Are,* though, Sendak expresses the wild, chaotic situations in verse. In fact, his shifts from prose to verse in the beginning and from verse to prose at the end mark the transitions to and from the fantasy world of the night kitchen.

The opening scene shows Mickey lying in bed in his room, and the narrator asks,

> Did you ever hear of Mickey,
> How he heard a racket in the night,
> And shouted QUIET DOWN THERE!

The language has no overtly regular rhythmic pattern, no metrical feet, and no parallel syntax in phrases. Nor does it contain rhyme. Thus Sendak chooses prose for the initial scene of Mickey's everyday world.

Yet in the opening illustration, while the narrator says, "Did you ever hear of Mickey, / How he heard a racket in the night," noises from "offstage" appear in comic-strip bubbles inside the picture—"THUMP," "DUMP," "CLUMP," "LUMP," and "BUMP"— suggesting the slapdash racket Mickey hears. With these pure rhymes Sendak introduces the first inkling of the chaotic world of the night kitchen.

Sendak handles the transition from Mickey's everyday world into his dream world in *Night Kitchen* the same way he does in *Wild Things,* controlling the greater intensity of wildness with a greater regularity of verse. After Mickey shouts "QUIET DOWN THERE!" and actually begins to fall toward the night kitchen in the illustrations, Sendak makes the rhythm of the narrative more patterned. The two phrases "fell through the dark, out of his clothes" repeat the same stress pattern with a definite lilt (DUM-ti-ti-DUM, DUM-ti-ti-DUM). The next lines shift from regular to random accents, but Sendak peppers the phrases with internal rhyme, alliteration, and assonance as Mickey falls "Past the moon & his mama & papa sleeping tight / into the light of the night kitchen."

Once the dream begins, the confusion increases, as does Sendak's use of verse. Describing the commotion, Sendak slips in a true rhyme, half-rhymes, and more alliteration, describing the night kitchen as a place

> Where the bakers who bake till the
> dawn so we can have cake in the morn
> mixed Mickey in batter, chanting.

Here "bake" rhymes with "cake"; "dawn" half-rhymes with "morn," as does "batter" with "chanting"; and the alliteration increases to the end of the lines from the phrase "bakers who bake" to "morn mixed Mickey." Though the stress patterns vary within the lines, the rhymes and alliteration tend to make the language sound more like verse than prose.

Once the fantasy is under way, Sendak increases his use of

verse by employing the rhythms of chants, thus further controlling the confusion of the dream. Placed intermittently throughout
the narrative, the chants create musical rhythm out of the chaos
in the night kitchen. The first chant appears immediately following the bakers' mistaking Mickey for milk, when the bakers chant
robustly,

> Milk in the batter! Milk in the batter!
> Stir it! Scrape it! Make it! Bake it!

When the bakers fear Mickey is going to abandon them, they
think the cake-baking is headed for calamity unless they get their
"milk" back. In a desperate rush they howl, "Milk! Milk! Milk for
the morning cake!" After Mickey successfully provides milk for
the bakers, they respond in their lengthiest song and dance yet,

> Milk in the batter! Milk in the batter!
> We bake cake! And nothing's the matter!

Not only are the bakers' chants musical in themselves, but they
together create a musical effect, echoing one another throughout
the narrative. All three chants repeat "milk," and the last of the
bakers' chants echoes the line of the first: "Milk in the batter!"
The focus of the confusion—the mistaking of Mickey for the
milk—thus receives the greatest quantity of verse in the text.

Mickey's language in the dream contrasts with that outside the
dream. Before entering the night kitchen, Mickey, on being dis-
turbed by the racket, shouts in prose, "QUIET DOWN THERE!"
After entering the jumbled world of the bakers, Mickey too speaks
in verse. Like the bakers' chants, Mickey's chants also concern the
mistaking of him for milk. "I'm not the milk and the milk's not
me!" he sings from the messy batter. And again, at the end of the
story when Mickey dives to the bottom of a colossal milk bottle,
relishing the confusion of himself for milk, he chants

> I'm in
> the milk
> and the milk's

in me.
God bless Milk
and
God bless Me!

This later chant mocks the earlier one by virtue of its similarity to it. Sendak repeats the same stress pattern in Mickey's first and last chants (DUM-ti-ti-DUM-ti-ti-DUM-DUM-DUM). Both chants make a statement and then reverse its order, as in "I'm not the milk and the milk's not me!" The repeated cadence and rhetorical pattern of the chants suggest that Mickey sings the same song with different verses. Again, the center of confusion—the mistaking of Mickey for milk—is the focus for the verse.

In one exception Mickey does not speak in chants during the fantasy, the reason perhaps lying in the situation. When in *Wild Things* Max tames the wild things and then takes complete charge of the situation, he speaks in prose; likewise, when Mickey calms the bakers by taking control of the situation, he too speaks in prose. When the bakers howl desperately, "Milk! Milk! Milk for the morning cake!" Mickey reassures them in prose:

What's all the fuss? I'm Mickey the pilot!
I get milk the Mickey way!

In contrast to his chants, this speech has random rhythm and the words do not rhyme. Yet whatever the reason for the exception, Mickey does not speak in chants before he enters the dream, whereas he and the bakers speak predominantly in chants throughout it.

As with the conclusion of *Wild Things,* Sendak ends *Night Kitchen* in prose. When the dream ends, the shift from verse to prose is so stark that the prose sounds like an epilogue:

Now Mickey in the night kitchen cried
COCK-A-DOODLE-DOO!
and slid down the side
straight into bed

cakefree and dried.
And that's why, thanks to Mickey
we have cake every morning.

The first sentence in verse accompanies Mickey's fall out of the dream and back into bed; the second in prose appears on the last page with a picture of Mickey. In contrast to the regular rhythm of DUM-ti-ti-DUM repeated in the three phrases "slid down the side," "straight into bed," and "cakefree and dried" and the end rhymes of "side" and "dried," the last two lines lack characteristics of verse. Consequently, the difference in sound and rhythm of the ending lines yields a sense of reasonability. These two lines oppose the nonsense connoted by Mickey's "COCK-A-DOODLE-DOO!" Offering the previous fantasy as a probable explanation for why "we have cake every morning," the last two lines effect a pedantic tone. Thus by beginning and ending the narrative in prose, Sendak creates boundaries around the fantasy, boundaries of setting and rhythm. In addition, he also achieves a difference in sensibility between the nonsense world and the prosaic one.

Appearing at the beginning and end of the picture book, when Mickey is not in the dream, the prose accompanies the world outside the dream, the everyday world of Mickey. The prose is appropriately informal for Mickey's everyday world. The narrator directly addresses the reader, asking "Did you ever hear of Mickey?" and at the conclusion explains "and that's why . . . we have cake every morning." With the pronoun "we" this final statement includes the listener in a casual, conversational style.

In contrast, the verse language associated with the fantasy sounds contrived. The sounds of the racket—"DUMP," "CLUMP," and "LUMP"—rhyme artificially; a real racket, by definition, has discordant sounds, not the harmonious ones of rhyme. The chants of "Milk in the batter! Milk in the batter" express dialogue not in a natural way but in a manipulated one. The artifice of the rhyme creates an imaginative sensibility appropriate for the imaginative action.

This change in sensibility also appears in the change in Mickey's language and attitude from first to last. In initially shouting

"QUIET DOWN THERE!" Mickey expresses the practical sensibility of a boy who has never visited the night kitchen and wants to get his rest. At the end of the story, however, Mickey's playful shouting of "COCK-A-DOODLE-DOO!" shows that his attitude toward the fantasy has changed from practical to participatory. Thus at the end, when Mickey falls out of the fantasy and back into bed, he sighs, "OH," "HO," "HUM," and "YUM." After experiencing the fantasy, Mickey now speaks in rhyme as he returns to his everyday setting. Because his language rhymes during the dream, as well as in this penultimate scene back in his bedroom, the rhymes suggest the merging of Mickey's everyday world with his dream world.

Outside Over There

Sendak arranges the rhythmic shifts in *Outside* differently from the way he does in *Wild Things* and *Night Kitchen*. In *Wild Things* he arranges the shifts to alternate between verse and prose because the narrative's focus alternates between wild situations and tame ones. In *Night Kitchen* he simplifies the rhythmic pattern to have prose at the beginning and end, with predominantly verse in the middle throughout the fantasy, so as to control Mickey's chaotic experience and turn it into a late-night song and dance in the kitchen. In *Outside* Sendak again shifts from the rhythm of prose to the rhythm of verse to control disturbing episodes for the protagonist; however, here he varies his rhythmic arrangement to be appropriate for Ida's own experience.

Ida's experience of wildness arises from her pressure to make the right decision. She feels torn between taking responsibility for her baby sister and at the same time not wanting to. DeLuca compares Ida's anxiety with the conflict frequently experienced among young girls who feel tension "between their desire to achieve for themselves and the demands placed on them to take care of others" (DeLuca 1984, 15).

Paralleling the fact that Ida's wrong choices cause her confusion in the story, Sendak expresses those episodes in which Ida makes wrong choices in verse and those in which she makes right choices in prose. Because Ida makes two wrong choices in the first half of the story, Sendak writes this first half predominantly in verse. In the second half of the story Ida makes the right decision, and so Sendak here uses prose in referring to her. Sendak, then, arranges the main rhythmic shifts from verse to prose in *Outside* to occur at the moments Ida makes right choices.

The first half of the book presents three episodes in which Ida makes choices. First, in the initial scene she chooses to ignore her baby sister. Sendak couches this opening sentence in predominantly iambic tetrameter:

> When Papa was away at sea,
> and Mama in the arbor,
> Ida played her wonder horn
> to rock the baby still—
> but never watched.

Each line of the opening sentence has a definite iambic meter except the third—"Ida played her wonder horn" switches to trochaic meter. This change of meter in the third line and the dash at the end of the fourth emphasize Ida's wrong choice: "Ida played . . . but never watched." Further, Ida's dilemma—to act responsibly or not—has emphasis because it opens the story.

Second, Ida chooses in the next situation to rescue her baby sister from the goblins but makes a "serious mistake." For this episode, Sendak composes the prelude to the mistake in the random rhythm of prose: "Now Ida in a hurry / snatched her Mama's yellow rain cloak"; however, he abruptly shifts to a verse rhythm in trochaic meter when Ida blunders and "[climbs] backwards out her window into outside over there." In this way Sendak deftly controls the painful mishaps in the story: when Ida is acting prudently, the rhythm is random; when, however, she is acting foolishly, the rhythm is steady.

Third, Ida's ability at the story's climax to make the right choice proves critical. Consequently, Sendak not only controls her anxiety with the rhythm of verse but makes the passage *look* like verse in stanzaic form:

> Foolish Ida never looking,
> whirling by the robbers caves,
> heard at last from off the sea
> her Sailor Papa's song:

> If Ida backwards in the rain
> would only turn around again
> and catch those goblins with a tune
> she'd spoil their kidnap honeymoon!

In the first stanza, the first two lines have a noticeable trochaic meter, and the last two switch to iambic meter. As Ida continues to move in the wrong direction, Sendak counters the disturbing effect with the rhythm of a song. Papa's song has consistent iambic tetrameter and use of end rhymes with "rain" and "again," "tune" and "moon." Sendak's choice to use precise rhythm and rhyme for this situation is significant because the scene of Papa's song marks both the literal and the moral "turning point" for Ida. Literally, Ida is traveling in the wrong direction; she must "turn around again and catch these goblins." Morally, Ida must direct all her energy toward responsible action; she has been neglectful in caring for the baby. The symmetry of the song controls the tension between Ida's wanting to obey her father and not wanting to look after her sister. The most verselike language in the narrative thus focuses on Ida and her toughest choice.

In the second half of the story Ida chooses rightly to win back her baby sister. Consequently, one hears the change in Ida reflected in the rhythm's change to prose. Sendak now uses random rhythm in the lines about Ida and verse rhythm only in the lines referring to the goblins, since they still choose to act rebelliously. The moment Ida enters the chaotic scene of the goblin wedding, Sendak refers to her in the random rhythm of prose:

so Ida tumbled right side round and found herself
smack in the middle of a wedding.

In the next lines, however, when the narrator switches focus to
the goblins' activity, a scansion of the lines shows a predominantly iambic stress pattern:

Oh, how those goblins hollered and kicked,
just babies like her sister!

Sendak has Ida respond in prose: "What a hubbub," she says. This
speech in prose directly contrasts with her former speech in verse
when she deliberately ignored the kidnapping ("'They stole my
sister away!' she cried, / 'To be a nasty goblin's bride!'"). Now Sendak makes it the goblins who chant in verse:

"Terrible Ida," the goblins said,
"We're dancing sick and must to bed."

Here Sendak omits words from the goblins' dialogue to make the
meter trochaic. He abbreviates the adverbial form from "sickly"
to "sick" in the phrase "we're dancing sick" and omits the word
"go" in the phrase "must to bed." To reinforce the true rhymes,
Sendak breaks the sentence at "said," making it appear as a
rhyming couplet. In short, within the longer passage the goblins'
speech not only sounds but also looks like verse.

After Ida rescues her sister, she returns home. As Ida nears
home, the change of rhythm in the narrative parallels her change
of setting from a fanciful goblin wedding to her home. The language increasingly takes on more characteristics of prose than
verse. At first, the sentence describing Ida's walk home has the
lilt of blank verse:

Now Ida glad hugged baby tight
and she followed the stream

that curled like a path
along the broad meadow.

The beginning phrases repeat the same stress pattern, ti-DUM,
ti-ti-DUM, as heard in "she followed the stream that curled like
a path along the broad meadow." But toward the end of the sentence, the phrase units become shorter and less lyrical, as Ida
walks "to her Mama / in the arbor / with a letter / from Papa, /
saying." These terse prepositional phrases create a choppy
rhythm whose unevenness resembles prose more than verse.

The final prose letter from Papa to Ida starkly contrasts with
the verse and rhyme of his previous song. He writes,

I'll be home one day,
and my brave, bright little Ida
must watch the baby and her Mama
for her Papa, who loves her always.

The uneven line lengths of the letter contribute to its uneven
rhythm, and although Papa uses alliteration in the descriptive
phrase "brave, bright," the passage is devoid of rhyme. As a result
of Papa's now speaking to Ida in prose rather than song, he emphasizes that she has returned from the land of dreams to the
ordinary world.

Sendak concludes *Outside* with one last line of prose referring
to Ida's response to her father's admonishment: when Papa writes
that Ida must watch the family for him, the narrator says that
this "is just what Ida did." DeLuca argues that the story's focus
on Ida's responsibility at the end never resolves the girl's initial
frustration (DeLuca 1984, 19). Keeping in mind, however, Sendak's rhythmic strategies throughout the rest of *Outside Over
There,* I have to conclude that because Sendak uses verse to express Ida's anxiety over watching the child in the beginning and
uses prose to indicate her freedom and control in obeying Papa in
the second half of the story, the employment here of prose is to
suggest that Ida assumes responsibility without anxiety. She matures. Thus Sendak, without altering the facts of Ida's everyday

world, wields his finely tuned rhythmic style to bring Ida's conflict to a reasonable, satisfying conclusion. Yes, she must still watch her baby sister—but Sendak suggests, in the relaxed rhythm of conversational prose, that Ida freely reconciles herself to that task.

Conclusion

Thus far I have presented Sendak's use of syncopated rhythm for his three picture books in fairly practical terms—as a means for managing children's troublesome feelings. Yet a particular romantic philosophy is also implicit in Sendak's merging jocund verse with fearful content: William Blake's artistic conviction that contraries be faced in life and expressed in art.

Throughout his poems from *Songs of Innocence and of Experience: Shewing the Two Contrary States of the Human Soul* (1794), Blake seeks to correspond unlike counterparts.[4] He includes poems of a meek lamb (Blake, 8–9) and a fierce tiger (24–25), a two-day-old smiling newborn (16) and another "Helpless, naked, piping loud; / Like a fiend hid in a cloud" (28). Yet as James Holt McGraven, Jr., notes, Blake does not merely polarize opposites; he offers an imaginative configuration of text and picture that transcends simple contrast and comparison. In his study of the Blakean counterpoint at work in Sendak, McGraven traces the way both artists play conflicting images and words off one another. Comparing Blake's illustrated poem "The Tyger" from *Songs of Experience* with *Wild Things,* McGraven writes, "Sendak's works indeed provide clear parallels to Blake's: discrepancies such as that between the terrifying but fascinating 'tyger' of Blake's poem and the anesthetized, almost stuffed look of the animal in the engraving recur in Sendak's 'wild things,' which in both text and illustrations seem simultaneously malignant and cuddly: 'We'll eat you up—we love you so!'"[5] Here McGraven notes the dialectic at work between Blake's verbal poem, which describes the tiger's eyes as fiery, and his graphic picture, which portrays those eyes in wide-open benignity, giving the big cat a doltish character. In like spirit, Sendak juxtaposes the contradictory content of roaring beasts in his text with their laughable overbites in his pictures.

Blake's vision of merged contraries philosophically undergirds Sendak's technique of shifting rhythms as well as the whole workings of each picture book. Sendak shifts his rhythms from verse or prose to counterpoint either the fearfulness of a word or the jocularity of an image. This use of syncopated rhythm is a single detail among many of how Sendak weaves a holistic worldview into the very fiber and frame of his art. In the picture books' counterpoints between words and pictures, goblins can simultaneously be foreboding, hooded figures and babbling babies. Bakers can be both comical, Oliver Hardy–style triplets and life-threatening henchmen at the oven door. As Blake's did, Sendak's art rebels against black-and-white polarites capturing the vibrant ambivalences of life.

7

Rungian Rhetoric and *Dear Mili*

In 1988 Michael di Capua published *Dear Mili: An Old Tale by Wilhelm Grimm,* illustrated by Maurice Sendak. The joint debut of Grimm's previously unpublished tale and Sendak's interpretive pictures proved to be a lucrative success. *Mili* leapt from the children's best-seller list to no. 9 on the adults' chart "for all hardback fiction soon after its release."[1] Some critics, however, felt that Sendak's illustrations contradicted Grimm's narrative. In two reviews critics took issue with Sendak's seemingly idiosyncratic embellishments. The writer and teacher Megan Anderson Bergstrom maintained that Sendak's pictures often opposed details in Grimm's narrative. For example, when Grimm portrays Mili as terrified, Sendak portrays her as calm and composed (Bergstrom, 52). And Janet Adam Smith noted that Sendak's visual interpretation went "far beyond the text," accusing Sendak of illustrating his "own fantasies" rather than focusing on Grimm's (Smith, 24, 26). She inferred that Sendak did not prepare himself as thoroughly for illustrating *Mili* as he had for illustrating the collection of Grimm's tales in *Juniper Tree* (24). I disagree, however, that the reason for Sendak's discrepancies with Grimm's narrative arises from any carelessness on his part; rather, I believe that Sendak characteristically illustrated *Mili* overzealously. Attuned to the counterpoint possible between word and picture in a picture book, Sendak, I feel, purposefully offset the tale's naive tone with an experienced view of life in his pictures to create a holistic worldview in *Mili*.

For such an ambitious undertaking, Sendak carefully chose both a contemporary and a colleague of Grimm as his chief visual inspiration—Philipp Otto Runge (1777–1810).[2] By comparing Runge's original paintings with Sendak's final version of them, I discovered that Sendak not only borrowed Runge's images but altered their original pious rhetoric to create his own vision of *Mili*.

Grimm's *Mili*

Like Runge, Grimm was a romanticist. In fact, both men belonged to the *Abendzirkel* (Circle of Intellectuals) who met to exchange ideas on German romanticism during its seminal period.[3] In Grimm's 167-year-old manuscript, he introduces his fairy tale in a letter to "Mili" that is stylistically romantic, with its melancholic tone and use of "pathetic fallacy," John Ruskin's later phrase for attributing human emotions to nature. Grimm begins by proposing that Mili has probably dropped a flower into a stream, not knowing that the flower would meet another tossed in by a child elsewhere. He continues that Mili has probably also witnessed a little bird flying away at dusk; she probably thought it was preparing for sleep. Actually, corrects Grimm, it was flying to meet another little bird "in the last ray of sunshine." The moral, explains Grimm, is that "the flowers and the birds come together, but people do not. . . . [T]hey have their set places and cannot be moved, and humans cannot fly. But one human heart goes out to another, undeterred by what lies between." Grimm fulfills that final dictum by sending his love to Mili through his ensuing story.

In contrast to the theme of his letter that human beings' lives are limited, the theme of Grimm's story concerns the miraculous overcoming of Mili's human limitations; an angel, saint, and God himself supernaturally intervene to shield the young girl from danger, loneliness, and even change. Mili, "a dear, good little girl," is living peacefully with her mother until war breaks out. Panicked, the mother sends Mili into the forest for protection, telling her, "God in His mercy will show you the way." Once alone in the forest, Mili grows terrified by the sounds of wild animals, birds, and wind in the fir trees. She prays, and a succession of miracles follows. Immediately, Mili is led out of the forest by her guardian angel and then guided to a well-lighted cottage by a fallen star. The cottage turns out to be the home of St. Joseph, who shelters the lost child for three days; in return, she prepares the meals. On the second day, a mysterious playmate appears for Mili, one whom Grimm reassures us is probably Mili's guardian angel. On the third day, St. Joseph foreshadows the concluding miracle to the tale by sending Mili home to her mother, handing her a rosebud, and promising that when it blooms she will return to him. Mili reaches her mother providentially through the escort of her angel. There she discovers that not three days but thirty years have elapsed. Incredibly, Mili has remained the same little girl, in the same rose-colored dress as when she parted from her home. Mili and her mother visit pleasantly in the evening; then St. Joseph's promise comes true: daughter and mother die together, with his rose "in full bloom" between them. Because of its "strong religious element, and goody-goody" verve, Smith likened *Mili* to "a story told in Sunday School" (24).

Runge's Rhetoric

Runge's art, however, is considerably more pious than Grimm's. Expressing his own brand of mystical Lutheranism, he spent his life working to develop a "new ideal, Classical, Romantic, Christian art" (Bisanz, 40). He attempted to do so by rejuvenating symbols from nature with his own private, religious meanings—a radical departure from the eighteenth-century pictorial tradition of painting historical subjects by classical standards. Runge assigned his own meanings to colors, plants, compositions for landscapes, and portraiture.

In Runge's scheme, specific colors offered specific messages to the viewer. Three of the primary colors stood for the Holy Trinity: blue represented God the Father; red, Christ his Son; and yellow, the Holy Spirit, or, in Runge's terms, "the solace granted us when red and blue have disappeared." The achromatic pair of white and black represented good and evil respectively.[4]

Further, particular plants articulated spiritual meanings for Runge. Oak trees symbolized the quintessential spirit of romanticism (Grundy, 49). The lily, the cornflower, and the nasturtium all unfolded as microcosms expressing "mysteries of the supernatural."[5] Specifically, Runge held that these geometrically formed flowers were the "purest form of the likeness of God" (Grundy, 69).

Runge transferred his emblematic conception of geometric patterns to his compositions. Perfect symmetry connoted unchanging order in his vision of art. As the art historian Robert Rosenblum comments, it was as "if some permanent truth that transcended the irregularities and casualness of the commonplace world had at last been disclosed" (Rosenblum, 45). To achieve such symmetry, Runge would scale his pictures not by empirical dimensions but by absolute geometric designs. Consequently, Runge enlarges the minutiae of flowers to unearthly dimensions and exaggerates the sense of distance in his picture plane. Rebelling against his classical training, he re-creates his own hierarchical scheme, based on the divine mysteries revealed to him through God's natural details (Rosenblum, 48–52).

The intensity of Runge's vision manifests itself in his portraiture. In the romantic tradition, the eyes of Runge's self-portraits unflinchingly confront the viewer's. The mood of these paintings is "weighty and brooding in their psychological charge" (Rosenblum, 63). In the portrait of his parents, Runge again fixes their stares directly into the audience's eyes (Rosenblum, 51).

More than simply showing them as romantic symbols of innocence, Runge presents children with the same detailed care he does plants—as "containers of natural mysteries" (Rosenblum, 53). In his portraits of children Runge intertwines the emblematic significances of their bodies with those of his flowers. Together, children and flowers convey an "organic energy" (Rosenblum, 52);

Rosenblum describes the appearance of the children's flesh as "pneumatic," bulging tautly over their muscles (51).

Closely associated with Runge's significance for the child is his meaning behind the winged *musizierender Genius,* or music-making cupid, that appears throughout his work (Grundy, 66). Because Runge's "artistic theory is anchored in his religious faith," these winged infants signify both actual angels and divine inspiration (Bisanz, 25). Runge's cupids incarnate the divine inspiration he deemed essential for creating art. Their wings connote that the inspiration they offer is fleeting; in fact, Runge believed that if an artist attempts to prolong the moment of mystical inspiration, it will leave him, departing as instantly as an angel (Grundy, 65). Runge almost always pictures these cupids in landscapes (Grundy, 65) because he "sought access to the supernatural . . . through the manifestations of the natural" (Rosenblum, 53).

The best way to understand Runge's iconography is to see it at work in one of his paintings. In *Die Lehrstunde der Nachtigall,* or *The Nightingale's Lesson,* Runge compares his method of composing this oil painting with a musician's approach to composing a fugue with theme and variations.[6] Runge sets an oval picture of Psyche and Cupid inside a larger, rectangular frame decorated with three winged cherubs and intertwining lilies, roses, and a live oak stump. In the inner picture Psyche also sits on a live oak branch; she focuses on Cupid positioned slightly above her in more branches and holding two tiny horns in each hand. Behind Psyche and Cupid in the shadows, another cherub slumbers on a crimson pillow.

In the narrow border rimming the oval, Runge has glossed the painting with the following poem by Klopstock:

> You must play the flute, sometimes with louder and louder tones, sometimes with softer ones, until the notes lose themselves; then blare it out, so that it rustles through the tree tops of the forest—play the flute, play the flute, until the notes lose themselves in the rosebuds. (Hohl, 164; trans. Rasch)

The poem concerns transcendence achieved through an abandonment to art ("[playing] the flute") and, in turn, that art enables earthly love, symbolized by the rosebuds.

Klopstock's poem partly explains Runge's private intent for his painting. Voicing the neoclassical standard for Runge's time, the art theoretician Johann Joachim Winckelmann mandated that the theme of Psyche and Cupid should follow the Greek's precedent denoting the artist's relationship to his muse. Reviving that neoclassical interpretation, Runge consciously personalized the Greek myth by creating an allegory of Psyche as his fiancée, Pauline; himself as Cupid; and the nature surrounding them as the artist's source for divine inspiration (Hohl, 163). Beginning the painting in 1801 and completing it in 1805, Runge felt that finishing the work paralleled consummating his love for his betrothed, or culminating their love in matrimony (Hohl, 163). Thus, in accordance with Klopstock's verse, Runge viewed his seeking perfection in his artwork as coinciding with his yearning for complete happiness with Pauline.

As in the style of a fugue, Runge uses the outer frame to repeat, embellish, and further develop the theme of his love for Pauline. There he abstracts the theme into his private iconography of cupids and flowers. At the top of the frame, a cupid plays a lyre on a living oak stump, a symbol of Runge's hope for eternal love. On the left, another cupid sits in a lily blossom, the symbol of perfection, completion, and thus eternity as well. Perched on his finger is a nightingale, the songbird of love. Couched in the petals of immortality, the cupid is able to listen intently to the bird's song. On the other side of the frame, still another cupid strains upward from a wild rosebud, a symbol for earthly love. This winged child reaches up with outstretched arms and hands to the nightingale above its head and beyond its reach. Runge expressed that the *Genius* of the rose yearns for love that can never be completely fulfilled on earth. The German art historian Hanna Hohl interprets this section of the painting with a letter from Runge to Pauline. It voices the separation Runge felt between a loving relationship on earth and one in heaven: body and spirit can be united only in paradise, he wrote, and then again in death (Hohl,

63). The nightingale compels Runge, or the artist, to aspire for true love here on earth but reminds him that perfect happiness is forever out of reach until eternity. The abiding focus, then, of Runge's artistic vision aims heavenward while still earthbound.

Sendak's Illustrations for *Mili*

In his own vision of *Mili* Sendak quotes Runge's images, yet he alters their premise from focusing on the divine to focusing on the human. Beginning with the book's dust jacket, Sendak transcribes images from *Nightingale*'s frame into his own comic key. Borrowing Runge's ornate arabesque of cupids, oak leaves, and flowers, Sendak parodies their tone playfully. Of Runge's three angels, Sendak chooses to copy only the posture of the cupid on the left who stares contentedly into the song of the nightingale, symbolizing perfection and immortality. He symmetrically positions this cupid on either side of the oval on his dust jacket. Sendak's rendition of the cupid emphasizes, however, not its perfection but its imperfections. Making his transformation clear, he alters the perfection of the cupid's physique to that of his own frumpy cherubs. He takes the sinewy body of Runge's *musizierender Genius* and renders his own cupids dumpily. Runge's angel has defined muscles on his arms and torso; Sendak's angels have flabby frames and dimples in their buttocks. In place of the taut wings on Runge's cupid, Sendak draws lumps of rounded feathers on his. The hair of Runge's cupid curls tightly into ringlets at the nape of his neck, while the hair of Sendak's cupids hangs in bedraggled fashion. Accordingly, Sendak consistently maintains his cartoon characterization of Runge throughout the frame by drawing his oak leaves with rounded edges instead of with Runge's naturalistic points. In short, Sendak's version makes light of Runge's, as his two pudgy cupids pose ceremoniously in the blooming fire lilies.

Given such stylistic alterations, it seems unreasonable to surmise that Sendak is attempting to paraphrase Runge's cosmogony here; if anything, Sendak burlesques it. In their comic flaws of lumpy feathers, limp hair, and flaccid figures, Sendak's cupids humanize Runge's idealized cherub. Rather than being manifestations of Runge's divine inspiration, Sendak's cupids incarnate his own wry wit.

Inside the oval of the dust jacket, Sendak assumes Runge's allegorical sensibility. Sendak's illustration of Mili and her mother emblematically allegorizes the journey of Mili in the longer narrative, yet it does not assume Grimm's saccharine tone; Sendak adopts the romantically contemplative mood of Grimm's prefatory letter. To illustrate Grimm's scenario from the letter, Sendak uses several images from different paintings by Runge that together produce a thoughtful, sobering effect. In the picture Mili and her mother stand arm in arm between a tree and a brook, contemplating a yellow rose. Paraphrasing the placement and line of Runge's undulating oak branch in *The Source and the Poet* (1805), Sendak frames the picture in a dark, shadowy line. In Runge's color scheme such darkness, as of the forest in the story, would indicate evil. In contrasting value Sendak's stream flows from a distant enclave of light through the shadow. In this way the waterscape allegorizes Mili's spiritual journey in the story, as she passes from the light of innocence through the dark woods of experience.

Following Runge's impulse for allegory, Sendak's rhetoric in his portrait of Mili works from a completely different understanding than Runge's in his depiction of children. As stated earlier, Runge viewed children as emblems of "organic energy," a quality he emphasized by drawing them in close correspondence to vigorous plant stems and stalks. Paraphrasing the blossoming white rose tree from Runge's *Rest on the Flight into Egypt* (1805–06), Sendak includes this plant in his introductory picture of Mili, yet he alters Runge's white roses to his own red ones, emblematic of earthly affection rather than divine love. In Runge's *Flight into Egypt* the cupid perches in the tree grasping a white bud. The juxtaposition of Runge's cupid's pneumatic flesh next to the blossoming flowers yields potent significances of energy, vitality, joy, and divine inspiration (Crown, 1990). Yet Sendak in his design blocks his child from any contact with the rose tree, positioning the adult between them. Accordingly, his child does not touch the rose in her mother's hand but instead stands woodenly, holding on to her mother. Characteristically, Runge sparked energy in his portraiture by creating eye contact between the subject and onlooker. In sharp contrast, Sendak draws both mother and child looking away from their audience. Through these details, then, Mili's figure exudes neither the intensity of Runge's children nor the exuberance of Grimm's. Sendak's Mili is burdensomely stiff; he portrays her with such staidness that it is difficult to believe she will actually be able to transcend her hardships as intimated by Grimm's ensuing narrative.

In the book's first illustration Sendak again secularizes Runge's artistic vision. Through his composition, he grounds the security of Mili in her earthly home instead of with any supernatural being. The first illustration pictures Mili and her mother, along with two dogs, sitting in front of their cottage. In the middle ground, a scrawny angel poses precariously among branches; in the background, a black cloud begins to loom above the woodland's tree line. In the stable design of a triangle, Sendak makes the head of Mili's mother form the apex as the dogs complete the other two corners, framing Mili safely inside. Moreover, he frames this smaller triangle securely inside a larger triangle outlined by the cottage roof. This tight configuration of mother and home emblematically shelters the figure of Mili.

Sendak's secure portrait of Mili differs slightly from the vulnerable picture of her that Grimm gives. Grimm's first sentence reads, "There once was a widow who lived at the end of a village; all she had in the world was a little house and the garden that went with it." His description emphasizes the scarcity of protection in Mili's home: she has no father; she lives on the outskirts; and the resources for her livelihood are minimal. He therefore places the family's hope for security in a heavenly source, concluding the scene by writing, "When danger threatened the little girl, she was always saved, and the mother often thought in her heart: My child must have a guardian angel."

To illustrate Grimm's stalwart guard, Sendak again alters Runge's image of an angel: he rejects Runge's idealized image of a cherub for the features of an everyday child. When Runge places his angels in trees, he balances them elegantly on the tip of a twig *(Nightingale),* lightly striking a harp in the boughs *(Source),* or settled symmetrically in the fork of the trunk *(Flight into Egypt).* In contrast, the whole design of Sendak's cupid is precariously asymmetrical. He wedges the top-heavy figure between willowy limbs, the angel's hand clinging above and his leg dangling below on the same side. As to proportion, the angel's stomach hangs roundly over skinny legs, as do the bulging bellies of real toddlers.

Sendak intensifies his design's rhetoric in the following illustration. With tongues of fire rimming black clouds in the background, Sendak reiterates the solidarity of Mili with her mother and the earthly childishness of the angel. Despite the mother's dramatic pose of extended arms and hands, Sendak still maintains her stable triangular lines for shielding Mili. The folds of the mother's skirt form a bold, triangular fortress that Mili holds onto and hides behind. In laughable fashion, the cupid in the tree shields his own eyes with one arm while braced to the tree with the other. Though the angel is to be religiously guarding Mili, here Sendak portrays him as preoccupied with his own welfare.

The following scene in Grimm's narrative is the pivotal episode in which the mother relinquishes being with Mili in order for God to protect the child completely. Grimm writes, "She took the child to the edge of the forest, kissed her, and let her go." Sendak embellishes this stark prose with a landscape from Runge and some pathos from Hollywood.

Likening his interpretation of Grimm's fairy tale to his childhood interpretation of the cinematic version of the great American fairy tale *The Wonderful Wizard of Oz,* Sendak here parallels the pathos of Dorothy's predicament in the witch's castle with Mili's at the edge of the forest. The helplessness of Mili's mother to protect her child echoes that of Aunt Em to rescue Dorothy—aunt and niece see each other in the crystal ball, but neither can control the situation. As a child, Sendak responded passionately to this scene in the motion picture. He explains, "I knew just what it meant, which was that a mother and child can be in the same room and want to help each other, and they cannot. Even though they were face to face, the crystal ball separated them. Something separates people now and then. And I think it's that moment that interests me, and compels me" (Rothstein, 16).

Censoring Runge's laurel-wreathed poet and music-playing angels from his *The Source and the Poet*, Sendak transforms Runge's jubilant landscape expressing the mysteries of God into his own dark scene stressing the limitation of Mili's mother to shield her daughter from harm.[7] He crops Runge's airy woodland to a dense thicket, one encroaching on Mili and her mother. Whereas the wavy oak branch extends high above the subjects' heads in Runge's landscape, in Sendak's it weightily hems in mother and child. Leaving a central opening in the wood as Runge does, Sendak alters its original value from light to dark. Calla lilies and irises delicately arch over a cupid playing a reed instrument in *Source;* for *Mili,* Sendak enshrouds his cupid in a thick bush. The cupid's formal pose inside the arched bush connotes the figure of an angel on a tombstone; now Sendak's guardian angel seems to be a harbinger of death, rather than a herald of life. The mood of Sendak's landscape serves as a tenebrous backdrop for the parting of Mili from her mother.

In emphasis, Sendak stages Grimm's drama in a human arena, focusing the illustration's tension between Mili and her mother. This aspect contrasts rhetorically with Runge's frequent schemes to create energy in his paintings through human beings' physical connections to divinely inspired nature. As noted earlier, Runge sought "access to the supernatural" through his landscapes (Rosenblum, 53) and thus depicted children exuding the same vitality and resiliency as those of the flowers they grasped (50–51). Sendak, in contrast, sparks emotional energy in his picture through the intense gaze of one human being into the eyes of another.

More important is that although Runge differentiates between the spirit of children and that of adults, Sendak portrays Mili with an attitude absorbed from her mother. In Runge's portrait of grandparents and children, *The Artist's Parents* (1806), Rosenblum notes the contrasts Runge draws between the couple and their two grandchildren (50): the grandmother holds a "plucked rose," while the children play with rooted, tough, blossomed stalks; the grandparents appear stern and rigid, while the children appear animated and energetic. Rosenblum feels that Runge is citing the difference between "the artificiality of the adult human world and the naturalness of a children's world" (51). In Sendak's illustration of Mili and her mother, he also formally parallels the adult and the child; however, his details link rather than separate the two figures. He dresses the woman and child in similar décolleté gowns of rosy hues, the color emblematically foreshadowing their final deaths together. He colors their hair identically. Most noticeable is that in sharp profile the facial expressions of mother and daughter mirror each other. Mili's restrained composure emulates her mother's. The worry in her eyes suggests she is not naive about the dark wood behind her. Gazing into her parent's eyes, she foresees the dangers her mother fears. Sendak interprets Mili with a burdened understanding of her situation—an insightful reading of Grimm's text, for, as Grimm proceeds with the story, he says that Mili's heart grew heavier.

In one of the book's two double spreads, Sendak portrays the moment in Grimm's text in which Mili finally becomes paralyzed by her fears: afraid of the wind, wild animals, sharp rocks, and creaking branches, she sits down, unable to continue, and cries, "Oh, dear God, help your child to go on." For his composition, Sendak quotes Mili's sitting position directly from Runge's *Nightingale*—in profile, Mili assumes Psyche's posture; like Psyche, Mili sits on a fallen oak tree and rests her feet on two offshooting branches, as if she were sitting on stairs, with one foot higher than the other. For his slumbering angel, Sendak also paraphrases the sleeping pose of Runge's cupid.

Runge, of course, is transposing the classical myth of Psyche and Cupid into his own vision. In the Greek myth the beautiful Psyche threatens the popularity of Venus, who, in secret revenge, arranges for her son, Cupid, to make the attractive maiden fall in love with a hideous serpent creature. Cupid, however, sees Psyche before he casts the spell and falls deeply in love with her. He then casts his own spell that prevents any other from falling in love with her. Unaware of either spell, Psyche's parents seek counsel from the gods regarding how to acquire a good match for their daughter. From the oracle, the parents learn of the irrevocable revenge of Venus: Psyche is destined to die in the arms of a monster-husband. She is sent alone to the top of a rocky cliff, where she fearfully awaits her fate. Unexpectedly, Cupid rescues her. Remaining invisible, he transports Psyche from the dark mountaintops to a refreshing meadow of flowers.

In *Nightingale* Runge reinterprets the moment of Psyche's transport in his own romantic notion of transcendence. His Psyche embraces the music-playing cupid with one hand and an oak bough with the other. Psyche, besides portraying Runge's fiancée, Pauline, expresses the dual inspiration from both a divine spirit and an empirical nature; however, Runge completely reorganizes his empirical view of nature into his own mystical scheme. He drastically manipulates the picture plane to balance the composition in perfect symmetry: in what looks like an inset, he renders a miniature waterfall in the lower right-hand corner; this lighted waterfall balances with the glowing cherub in the upper left-hand corner; and across this diagonal line he positions the diagonal line formed by Psyche's figure. In Runge's scheme the rhetoric of such a symmetrical composition connotes order and absolute truth. Complementing his re-created Cupid and landscape, Runge gives Psyche her own wings to rise above the earthly into a spiritual realm.

Sendak's version rejects Runge's blissful gloss of the Greek myth; instead, he resurrects the terrifying tone of the Greek Psyche's solitary night on the hilltop. Pictorially, Sendak has Mili pass through the "valley of the shadow of death." In his rendition Mili does not transcend suffering—she contemplates it. Embellishing Grimm's catalog of natural terrors (wind, wild beasts, and screeching hawks), Sendak's interpretation suggests the horrors people can inflict on one another.

Specifically, in his German landscape Sendak recalls the terrors of the Jewish Holocaust.[8] In the distance he pictures a structure resembling a concentration-camp watchtower. That this building is indeed a concentration camp for Jews can be inferred from the graves marked with the Lion of Judah, the Star of David, and the Hebrew script Sendak pictures later in the story. Sendak displays the carnage of war through his anthropomorphic forest. He draws the gnarled tree trunks and fallen branches as if they were emaciated corpses and knotty human limbs. To the far left, a gray, split tree trunk forms the indubitable shape of a headless body with strained torso, hips, thighs, and calves. Below it, mustard limbs stretch out as skeletal appendages. The ghoul-like characters crossing the bridge may suggest workers from the camp, portraying the living dead.[9] Pitting Mili against such a backdrop, Sendak parallels the little girl's pilgrimage with the situation of those who had to suffer innocently for their faith. He confronts Mili, and the viewer, with the suffering of humanity incarnate in the skeletal rubble.

In the following episode Sendak supposedly illustrates an encouraged, consoled Mili, one Grimm describes as "lighter at heart" and "easy in her mind." Yet in the illustration Sendak does not focus on Mili; he places the angel at center stage, beneath a Rungian blossoming rose tree. In Runge's *Flight into Egypt* his blossoming white rose tree studded with cupids symbolizes both the innocence and the energy of the Blessed Virgin and the Christ Child; however, as one critic points out, the tree reflects, more than these religious meanings, the ability of Runge's landscape to communicate the transcendent feelings of the human soul.[10] In this vein Sendak's images of the rose tree with child and cupid resting beneath it seem to parallel the whimsical tone of Grimm's text. Nonetheless, the sensibility of Sendak's images differs from that of Runge's, with Sendak picturing Runge's images in a worldly rather than otherworldly light in his characterization of the guardian angel.

At the most, the characterization of Mili is ambiguous. In the preceding forest scene, Sendak pictures her worried and stunned. Under the rose tree, Mili relaxes, her legs spread out in front of her. But because Sendak does not show her face, her own mood remains unverifiable.

Further, Sendak's alteration of the angel's portrait upstages the child. Sendak profiles the cupid's face, which has suddenly taken on manly rather than boyish characteristics. The cupid's formerly straight hair has become meticulously marcelled into regular waves. His musculature is now defined. His wingspan is wider and stronger, and the grip of his hand is sure against the tree trunk. Most notably, Sendak has aged his facial features. Sendak shows a dark circle under his eye and a larger nose. The look in his eye is no longer impish; it is now pensive and questioning. Given the sudden maturity of the cupid and his position between Mili's feet, Sendak implies Mili's coming-of-age with these emblems connoting sexuality.

Repeatedly, Sendak presents Mili with reserve, countering Grimm's effusively emotional picture of her. When Grimm describes Mili as going outside "happily," amazed at the lovely garden surrounding St. Joseph's cottage, Sendak draws her standing erect, left arm straight at her side, eyes down, her right hand tentatively touching a huge Rungian fire lily—an oversized blossom that in Runge's cosmogony imparts vigor and raw energy to any child who touches it. In Sendak's scheme, Mili seems unaffected; her most animated characteristic is the inanimate blue ribbon tied to her hair. When Grimm describes Mili encountering her guardian angel for the first time, Sendak shows her surprise with the same controlled gesture with which he showed her fear in the forest—she holds her hand to her cheek. On the third day, when Grimm says that Mili and her angel "played together in pure joy and glory," Sendak stifles the intense, breathless play of children and instead pictures the two girls woodenly side by side, their arms around each other, with no facial expressions viewable. Then near the end of her adventure, when Mili travels home, Grimm writes that she "grew so tired that she had to stop." Here Sendak depicts the immediately ensuing moment, when the angel's flower potion supposedly revives the exhausted girl. But in this alleged moment of invigoration, Sendak again suppresses the energy in the scene, posing the angel artificially with an empty gesture. In the book's final double spread, Sendak has Mili walk toward her mother, ceremoniously holding the long-stemmed rose in front of her like a bridesmaid, sedate and serene. Only her feet move; the rest of her remains quiet. Instead of imparting vitality to Mili, the rose subdues her demeanor. Here

Mili's portrait may parallel that of the grandmother who holds the "plucked rose" in Runge's *Artist's Parents*. If so, Sendak acutely collapses Runge's symbol for life and vigor—the child holding the flower—into his own lyrical emblem for death. The combined effect of Grimm's blissful description and Sendak's sobering picture presents a child well beyond her years in understanding. Neither depiction cancels out the other; together they present a child capable of trusting unreservedly in a benevolent Creator while experiencing the strains of life.

For a closing example, I wish to look at Sendak's illustration for the parting of Mili from St. Joseph. Several of Sendak's embellishments here suggest his artistic vision for the whole tale. In the romantic tradition of portraiture, Sendak pictures the German shepherd peering directly into the eyes of the viewer. Throughout the pictures of Mili's stay with St. Joseph, Sendak presents the gradual aging of this dog. In this final illustration, the dog confronts the viewer with the fact that time has been passing. Coinciding with the dog's aging, Sendak's moon has waxed: when Mili first arrived at St. Joseph's, it was a slender crescent; now it shines bright and full. Something magical is happening according to Sendak's rhetoric but not necessarily in the supernatural realm Runge and Grimm aspired to. Sendak's mist, a pictorial convention for mystical experience, appears heavy and solid; it does not evoke the ethereal sensibility of Runge's mists. Instead, Sendak's emblems of mist, moon, and dog connote the human sequence of changing and growing old; such survival is a miracle in itself, though not an otherworldly one. Here Sendak unfolds the story of Mili using emblems that belie the nature of humanity defined ultimately by death. By tempering the innocent tone of Grimm's tale with such realism, Sendak portrays a child who because of her faith cannot transcend her trials but who can endure them.

Conclusion

Viewing Sendak's pictures for *Dear Mili* is strikingly similar to deciphering a medieval palimpsest: the one piece of vellum holds layers of passages written at different times and incompletely erased, and the reader, in scrutinizing the old parchment, notices remnants of other texts bleeding through to the surface. Likewise, in "reading" the illustrations for *Dear Mili* the viewer can decipher not only Sendak's illustrations but also the images of Runge's below the surface. I contend that, unlike interpreting the latest writing on the palimpsest, which makes no reference to the writings beneath it, interpreting Sendak's final illustrations for *Mili* demands that the reader take Runge's previous pictures into account.

Without a visual literacy in Runge, the viewer may understandably interpret Sendak's somber portrait of Mili as contradictory to Grimm's lively description. But considering the previous discussion of Runge's rhetoric, I conclude that, though Grimm and Sendak differ on certain physical details, they are actually working from the same romantic, melancholic understanding that Runge intended for *Nightingale*—that is, that perfect happiness is beyond the reach of human beings while they are still on earth. Grimm intimates this melancholic notion in his prefatory letter to the tale; however, consistent with the genre limitations for a folktale, he portrays Mili as a "one-dimensional" character—the "good, little girl."[11] As an insightful counter to Grimm's flat characterization of Mili, Sendak rounds out Grimm's sometimes-naive portrait with pictures expressing Mili's keen understanding and somber contemplation. He presents her in his pictures as a thoughtful child capable of yearning for happiness beyond what she experiences. The brevity of Grimm's text, another stylistic limit of the folktale (Stewig, 209), condones, even demands, Sendak's embellishments and interpretive details for the story. In the whole context of *Mili* as a nineteenth-century German romantic folktale, then, Sendak perceptively develops Grimm's character by highlighting the tension between what she experiences (suggested by his pictures) and what she believes (suggested by Grimm's words).

My view that Sendak counterpoints the author's words in his illustrations to better express the author's spirit for those words was played out in a much earlier Sendakian performance. When Sendak deviated from an author's text in the past, he did so thoughtfully to maintain the author's attitude toward the subject. In 1963, illustrating *The Griffin and the Minor Canon,* Sendak altered Frank Stockton's verbal portrait of the griffin from having a serpent's tail to having the backside of a lion and offered the following rationale for taking such a liberty. "Being an illustrator who does not arbitrarily deviate from a text," he wrote in the preface, "I feel obliged to give my reasons for doing so."[12] Sendak then explained that in staying true to Stockton's regal characterization of the imaginary creature—"strong, proud, imperious . . . and, best of all, lion-hearted"—he felt compelled to fashion the beast with powerful legs and tail. He noted, "Such a creature loses in dignity when his body dwindles weakly into a serpent's tail" ("About," 5).

This anecdote parallels Sendak's treatment of Grimm's angel for *Mili.* His choice to replace Grimm and Runge's pious vision of angels with a sometimes-comic one ironically maintains a fitting sensibility for the divine as the peculiar. Like William Blake, who would have recoiled from the artificial polarities of "secular" and "religious," Sendak through his humorous characterization portrays a guardian angel for Mili that may be more purely empathetic with her then a stereotypically, idealized cherub could be. Consequently, as a seeming contradiction to Grimm's traditional piety, Sendak offers a glimpse of an angel who at times seems more human than Mili herself. Sendak's winged toddler surprises the viewer with a human picture of a celestial bodyguard in the same spirit of surprise Clarence holds for George Bailey in Frank Capra's 1946 film *It's a Wonderful Life.*

Finally, it seems that I have excused Sendak of all the initial charges against him concerning *Mili.* I have explained his discrepancies with Grimm's text for the portrait of Mili as his use of artistic license to capture better the true spirit of the text; I have explained his use of a comic flair for the angel as a keen way of capturing the peculiar nature of the divine. I would even go so far as to suggest that his embellishments of his own personal details—the name of his dog Io on a grave marker at the end; the name of his mother, Sadie, on a tombstone; the scene of the wigged man directing the children's choir—all further rather than prohibit the reader's interest in the story, simply because they engage the reader as an active interpreter.

Yet what I cannot excuse, and what I feel prevents *Mili* from being one of Sendak's finest works, is the unevenness of his portraiture. His inability to depict the same character with a consistent likeness is a flaw usually associated only with his very early works (as is Grandpa's portrait in DeJong's *Shadrach*). But in *Mili* the girl's physical features change with almost every appearance. Her first profile, struck while she clings to her mother's skirts, fails to mirror either of her profiles in St. Joseph's garden—the pictures could be of three different girls. Likewise, the mother's cartoonish figure on the opening page bears little resemblance to Sendak's picture of the woman for the edge-of-the-wood episode. It is unfortunate that such inconsistencies mar a picture book with so rich an artistic vision.

8

Sendak's Legacy

"His early popularity notwithstanding," writes Selma Lanes, "Sendak has at no time during his career been in step with the mainstream of American children's book illustration" (Lanes, 51). Here Lanes is referring to Sendak's style. She points out that when illustrators were using bright colors and abstract designs in the midfifties, Sendak was experimenting with crosshatching techniques from the nineteenth century (51). Of more notoriety, Sendak's stylistic penchant for contraband subject matter earned him the dubious honor of being the cover feature for *Rolling Stone*.[1] Assuming the tone for a tabloid, Jonathan Cott headlined the article with the quips "Cannibalism? Doggie poop? Little flying kids with their 'wild thingies' showing? In children's books? Apparently so, because Maurice Sendak is their most popular author/illustrator in America today" (Cott, 5). Were Cott's sensationalism all there is to Sendak, he would be, as Jill May put it, "worthy only of witty cocktail party banter."[2] Sendak's abstinence from bowdlerizing, however, stems from his conviction that all his books must excel artistically. For Sendak, valuable art offers a true "sense of life" in an imaginative form (*C&C*, 74). By painstakingly honing such art, Sendak has evolved from renegade to veritable paragon in the picture-book industry.

Influence on Critics

Appropriate Subject Matter

Though perhaps biased, Michael di Capua, Sendak's editor at Farrar, Straus, and Giroux, summarizes Sendak's career by claiming that Sendak "turned the entire tide of what is acceptable, of what it is possible to put in children's-book illustration. There is nobody to compare with Maurice."[3] Di Capua's accolade also serves as a telling comment for why Sendak's art was not as readily welcomed by other critical readers—they deemed his work inappropriate for children. Sendak championed the issue of such appropriateness by presenting his subjects honestly. It is thus interesting to chronicle how his most successful books were also his most controversial ones.

Wild Things raised its ruckus in 1963; *Night Kitchen*, in 1970. Some critics, however, realized that Sendak's candor was essential for the cathartic effect of both books. As the art critic Brian O'Doherty notes, Sendak tries to present children as they are, rather than as they "ought to be" (Braun, 37). Through the art of Mickey's fantasy, Sendak channels what might be destructive feelings associated with sexuality into redeeming ones. In another review, Sada Fretz explains, "Just as *Where the Wild Things Are* offered a safe outlet for feelings of anger and aggression (and alarmed many adults), *In the Night Kitchen* celebrates childhood sexuality—or at least, with all the kneading and pounding and the naked immersion in milk, dough, and cake batter, sensuality" (Kloss, 573).

Applying psychoanalytic theory to *Night Kitchen,* Robert Kloss takes Fretz's interpretation a step further, positing that part of Mickey's anger in the beginning can be attributed to his "primal fantasy" of being excluded from his parents' enjoyment of sexual intercourse (573). Granted, such an interpretation relies on reading Freud's theories into Sendak's personal narratives as well as the story itself. And as Kloss concedes, the noise that awakens Mickey comes not from the parents' bedroom but from the Oliver Hardy–type bakers downstairs in the night kitchen. Thus, in Kloss's final estimation the playful mood of the book "removes the sexuality from the realm of anguish and anger and transposes it to one of comedy and pleasure" (574). The book's tone certainly supports both Fretz's and Kloss's interpretations that a child's sense of physical experiences can be playful and joyful.

The year after *Night Kitchen*'s debut, Sendak began illustrating a collection of Grimm fairy tales entitled *The Juniper Tree*. He did not censor his illustrations, because he felt the Grimm brothers did not bowdlerize their tales. "The Grimm tales are about the pure essence of life—incest, murder, insane mothers, love, sex—what have you," said Sendak (Commire, 27: 194). Again some critics called into question the book's suitability for children. In giving his rationale Sendak redefined his audience, arguing that historically a good story was read by young and old alike—not just by the former. "There was a time in history when books like *Alice in Wonderland* and the fairy tales of George MacDonald were read by everybody," he said. "They were not designated as being 'for children'" (Commire, 27: 194). In his review of *Juniper Tree* William Anderson identifies Sendak's widening audience as a pivotal contribution to the field. He writes, "A major benefit of Sendak's work has been a new survey of older boundaries of children's literature, resulting in a healthy sense that children's literature is not really separate from adult literature after all."[4] Ironically, in contrast to others' squeamishness at *Juniper Tree,* Anderson found Sendak's illustrations disappointing in their "inability to evoke either evil or brooding malevolence" (Anderson, 216).

In essence, Sendak had done such a good job of influencing professional critics that when *Dear Mili,* another Grimm fairy tale, premiered in 1988, among its chief criticisms was Jane Adam Smith's view that Sendak's illustrations were "pretty" instead of brooding (26). Of less import, Smith facetiously pointed out that also disappointing was Sendak's censoring of the naked cupid's lower anatomy (26). She concluded that *Dear Mili* is too charming to capture the "psychic reality" of the German fairy tale (24).

Book Design

In the early 1960s Sendak faced a generation that did not view the picture book as a genre distinct from the illustrated book. A decade later, scholars in children's literature were beginning to define the difference. In their preface to *The Child's First Books* Donnarae MacCann and Olga Richard gave textbook definitions for the two genres, defining an illustrated book as one "which may have many illustrations or decorations on its pages but still [have] a clear predominance of text" and a picture book as one "in which the written narrative is brief and the story line or other content is largely presented through illustrations."[5] In other words, picture books rely on the interdependence of words and pictures to tell the whole story. Such a tightly woven art form places high demands on the artist, an element Sendak's audience was for the most part unaware of.

In 1963 a librarian named Mai Durham summed up the contemporary plight of the picture-book genre.[6] Appalled by the lack of sensitivity to book design and artistic quality in picture books, she pronounced that a picture book should have "substance in text, aesthetic interpretation through illustrations, and harmonious book design" (Durham, 480). She criticized illustrators for being reluctant to try fine- and especially modern-art styles. She noted, however, that a well-crafted style was not in itself enough—paramount was that the words, pictures, and whole design of the book work together. Emphatically, she cited the best picture-book era as that of the Victorians, with such masters as Crane, Greenaway, and Caldecott. This was the call to arms that Sendak had already heard and answered, for in that same year he premiered *Where the Wild Things Are* and in the next year won the Caldecott Medal.

In Sendak's 1964 acceptance speech for the Caldecott Medal, he shared his philosophy, gleaned mainly from the works of Caldecott, of what a picture book should be and do. He stated that "the single element" accounting for Randolph Caldecott's greatness was "music and dance" (*C&C*, 145). Here Sendak is speaking on two levels, both metaphorically and literally. Metaphorically, he is referring to the technical interdependence of illustrations and text to share the narrative of the whole book—a concept that is the most important standard Sendak has brought to the forefront of the picture-book genre. Literally, Sendak is describing the frequency with which Caldecott drew characters singing and dancing. "No one in a Caldecott book ever stands still," elaborated Sendak. "If the characters are not dancing, they are itching to dance. They never walk; they skip" (*C&C*, 146).

And yet it is not simply these jovial images of Caldecott's that appeal to Sendak; he admires most the man's genuine spirit. As Sendak wrote in "The Shape of Music," "In terms of technique, it is no difficult matter for an artist to simulate action, but it is something else to *quicken,* to create an inner life that draws breath from the artist's deepest perception" (201).

The critics welcomed Sendak's restatement of Caldecott's practice of the picture-book art form. Yet somewhat rigidly, certain of them adopted Sendak's style as the inspired version of how a picture book should be done. In short, Sendak's picture books began to establish the rules for other picture books. As a case in point, at the Second Biennale of Illustrations in Bratislava, Yugoslavia, in 1969, the international children's book critic Horst Kunnemann delivered a challenge to illustrators for producing higher quality of work.[7] He cited Sendak's *Wild Things* as an exemplary model, praising Sendak's illustrations for their "overpowering style of the 19th century, [evoking] fear coupled with an understanding of psychology, the child's spirit and of art" (Kunnemann, 70). Citing 10 "exemplary" books in all, Kunnemann stated that other picture books should be "evaluated" by them (65).

At the time, some critics were doing just that—comparing others' work with Sendak's for evaluative purposes. Mercer Mayer, who also enjoys drawing monsters for children, tells the humorous story of *There's a Nightmare in My Closet*'s bittersweet reception among critics when they compared it with Sendak's *Wild Things:* "[The critics] tore [*Nightmare*] to shreds, and turned 'My Nightmare' into a best seller. There was so much negative said about it, that it got enough people interested in taking a look at it."[8] Even as late as 1985, Paul Arakelian was still comparing the two books and finding Sendak's better.[9] Arakelian favors Sen-

dak's work because the "entire enterprise—text, drawings, printing, story—becomes one metaphor for Max's going and coming"
(Arakelian, 126). This is Caldecott's criterion that Sendak reiterates: that the whole design of a picture book work together.

A quick review of Sendak's honors from numerous and varied
critics of children's literature would make one suppose that he
had been an instant success. From 1952 through 1973 Sendak's
illustrations for other writers gleaned his work the New York
Times Choice of Best Illustrated Book of the Year almost an-
nually; in 1964 Sendak won the Caldecott Medal for *Where the
Wild Things Are;* in 1970 he was the first American to receive the
Hans Christian Andersen Award (which he christened the "Hans
Jewish Andersen" [Braun, 42]. This last award, given for the entire body of his illustrations, bestowed on Sendak the "highest
international honor for excellence in the illustration of children's
books" (34); and in 1990, the Youth Services Section of the New
York Library Association christened Sendak as the first recipient
of its Empire State Award for Excellence in Literature for Young
People.[10] Academics too have applauded Sendak's expertise with
their own kinds of accolades: In 1977 Boston University presented him with an honorary doctorate in Humane Letters; in
1981 the University of Southern Mississippi awarded him its de
Grummond Collection Medallion; in 1984 Princeton University
gave him the honorary degree of Doctor of Fine Arts introducing
him as the person who "has delayed bedtime for thirty-seven
years."[11]

Influence on Authors and Illustrators

Though perhaps such success could engender a competitive, snob-
bish attitude, Sendak continually helps other artists achieve in
the field. He sees the children's book industry as difficult to break
into: "It's so much tougher today than when I started out," he
confides (Clemons, 52). Consequently, he has made a lifelong
commitment to helping younger artists get started.

As soon as Sendak established himself by winning the Caldecott in 1964 for *Wild Things,* he immediately began sharing both his influence and his philosophy of the art of the picture book to help others enter the field. Writer Jan Wahl (b. 1933) was able to get recognition for his first published story, *Pleasant Fieldmouse,* through Sendak's illustrating it in 1964. When Wahl told Ursula Nordstrom, Sendak's and his editor at Harper & Row, that he wanted Sendak to illustrate for him, she agreed and so did Sendak.[12] From this initial advantage, Wahl has gone on to write some 75 other books for children. Moreover, Sendak's collaboration with Wahl was fruitful because it opened an avenue for the two to share their philosophies on the art of the picture book, particularly regarding the importance of a sense of movement. Wahl, Sendak, and later another picture-book artist, Uri Shulevitz (b. 1935), have compared the way a picture book works to how an animated cartoon does (Sarkissian, 3: 301).

Sendak has directed Shulevitz most markedly in terms of picture-book layout. The influence of the older artist's design of *Wild Things* comes through in the younger artist's design for *One Monday Morning* (1967). Although Sendak structures *Wild Things* as a journey from the everyday world to a fantastic one and back, while Shulevitz structures *Monday Morning* as the constant switching back and forth between an everyday setting and an imaginary one, both artists use the visual metaphor of the pictures' increasing and decreasing in size to parallel the protagonist's imaginative journey. *Wild Things* is famous for its layout of pictures that widen from small blocks to three double spreads and then gradually diminish, corresponding to the imaginative intensity of Max. Shulevitz's layout mirrors this design except that he uses circular pictures that widen in the beginning and diminish at the end. Besides expanding the picture frames, both artists heighten the subjects inside the frames. Just as Sendak enlarges the size of his characters to intensify Max's fantasy, so too does Shulevitz accompany his story's climax with increases in the size of his imaginary characters: where Sendak's enormous wild things crowd the double-spread rumpus scene, Shulevitz's royal figures grow to gargantuan proportions as they all crowd into the little boy's room in *Monday*'s climax.

Also both artists employ the same technique to show how the little boy's imagination works. Sendak and Shulevitz include a hint of the imaginary world in the everyday one. For example, Sendak previews the lumbering wild things' entrance to Max's imaginary world by hanging in Max's family's stairwell a picture of one of them drawn by Max. He also uses remnants of the imaginary world in the ordinary setting by making Max's plant grow into a jungle and his bedposts into a forest. Shulevitz holds his link between the two worlds until the end of his picture book, when the king, queen, prince, and all the members of their court reappear on the boy's deck of cards. Shulevitz also posts a suspiciously royal-looking doll in the window of the toy store on the boy's street. In his later picture books, as the new day brightens gradually in *Dawn* (1974) and the journey extends in *The Treasure* (1978), Shulevitz, like Sendak, uses a variety of styles, in his formats of arranging pictures and text to parallel the story metaphorically.

Sendak imparted a more formal influence on a protégé when he taught a course in picture books at Parsons School of Design in New York. There Sendak met and taught the then-aspiring illustrator Richard Egielski (b. 1952), who credits Sendak with committing him to the art of the picture book: "Maurice Sendak was the most important teacher I ever had. In my opinion, a teacher can't really do that much for you technically. That's something you have to do for yourself. . . . An important teacher is one who exposes you to something new, and points out a direction you otherwise might have missed. In introducing me to the art of picture books, Maurice Sendak became a crucial influence. The quality of his work is a continuing inspiration."[13] As with Wahl and Shulevitz, Sendak again shared more than a technique with Egielski; as his mentor, he shared his philosophy of the importance of rhythm and music in the visual pleasure of a child's book.

For his own work, Egielski prioritizes many Sendakian creeds for creating picture books. Like Sendak, he believes the excellence of the text comes first to prompt excellence in the illustrations—and one criterion of "an excellent text" is its sense of rhythm and texture of language (Commire, 49: 94). And just as Sendak listened to *The Magic Flute* while composing *Outside Over There,* so too does Egielski like to listen to music as he draws, though his muse is not Mozart but the more recent Brian Eno (49: 96). Commenting on the influence of his mentor, Egielski confesses, "Sometimes, I feel like I'm writing music—visual music, that is. The picture book form is very musical: reading the words, looking at the pictures, turning the pages all make a rhythm" (49: 95).

Egielski graduated from Sendak's tutelage to illustrate prize-winning picture books: *Louis the Fish* was selected as the *School Library Journal*'s "Best Book of the Year" for 1980; *It Happened in Pinsk* won the Plaque from the Biennale of Illustrations in Bratislava in 1985; and *Hey, Al* won the Caldecott Medal for best picture book of 1987. In 1988 Scholastic Inc. published *Sing a Song of Popcorn: Every Child's Book of Poems,* featuring illustrations by nine Caldecott Medal winners. Here Egielski's work appears under the same cover as his former teacher's; now they are colleagues.

This small sampling of the body of Egielski's triumphs cites books reflecting collaborations with another young writer influenced by Sendak, Arthur Yorinks (b. 1953). In fact, Sendak got the artist and writer together.

When Arthur Yorinks was 16 and in the throes of adolescent idealism, he thought he would ask Maurice Sendak to look at some of his stories. As Yorinks puts it, "I showed up at Maurice Sendak's door unannounced" (Commire, 49: 213). Facing Sendak's doorbell, Yorinks panicked; he dismissed his gumption and turned to leave but not before Sendak had opened the door. That opened door was to be the first of many. Later, when Yorinks had his first children's story accepted by Farrar, Straus, and Giroux but had no illustrator for it, Sendak suggested the perfect artist— Richard Egielski. Yorinks and Egielski met and realized the genius of Sendak's judgment. "Maurice has been a big help and a constant inspiration," says Yorinks. "I still think he is the contemporary standard for picture books and children's literature in general" (Commire, 49: 213).

In 1988, the year after Yorinks and Egielski won the Caldecott

Medal together for *Hey, Al,* the actor Robert Redford asked Sendak to come and serve as artistic director for his newly christened Sundance Children's Theater, whose purpose was "to develop young talent" (Clemons, 52). Sendak, eager to encourage budding artists, accepted. "My great editor at Harper, Ursula Nordstrom, who died this year [1988], was able to bring me along gradually," Sendak comments. "I'd like to do that for others" (52).

Influence on Children

Ironically, the population Sendak has probably most influenced is the one who he claims remains the least impressed by his success—children. "The great virtue of children," notes Sendak in a 1986 interview, "is that they don't understand success and they write you with a candor and harshness that adults can't conceive of. They remain an honest audience, totally unimpressed by you—and they tell you."[14] Sendak describes how children, his "best critics," as he refers to them, critique his books: "When children love your book, it's 'I love your book, thank you, I want to marry you when I grow up.' Or it's 'Dear Mr. Sendak: I hate your book. Hope you die soon. Cordially'" (*C&C,* 214). That Sendak's books evoke such impassioned responses from their readers belies partly the nature of the readers but also the nature of Sendak's books: they are engaging enough to beckon such strong involvement.

Sendak tells the story of receiving an angry letter from a young girl in Canada in response to *Outside Over There.* She hotly informed Sendak that she did not like his book "at all" because "it scared her and she didn't like being scared." Then, in a postscript she elaborated that her mother, on reading the letter, deemed it too harsh. Accordingly, for 10 more pages the young reader explained how the goblins frightened her. Sendak considers her one of his best critics because she reconsidered her position thoughtfully for him. In the end, she decided that instead of being afraid of the goblins, she merely pitied them—"because," as Sendak retells her case, "they were babies. And these were babies who didn't fit into their clothes." The young girl decided that since these ill-clothed goblins must have been poor, it was disrespectful of her to loathe them. At the close of the lengthy letter was yet another note—this one from the girl's mother, who explained to Sendak that her daughter had recently been joined by a new baby sibling "and that a lot of soul-searching had been going on since then."[15] The child had encountered a bit of her own life in Sendak's picture book, and the honesty of his art compelled her own frankness.

Yet not all children are engaged by Sendak's work through being angry at him; some are simply curious. In "The Child and the Picture Book: Creating Live Circuits" Barbara Kiefer describes her study of listening for 40 weeks to children's responses to picture books.[16] She is convinced that the picture-book medium offers the child an active way of knowing. At a Columbus, Ohio, alternative elementary school, Kiefer witnessed several lively encounters with Sendak's *Outside Over There*. The fugal network of verbal narrative and plot illustration accompanied by subplots in the illustrations called on the children's imaginative resources to decide how all three lines of narrative were related. The children were especially intrigued by the subplots. According to some fourth-graders, "the storm depicted through the window as Ida discovers the baby's absence represents the heroine's true feelings—'She has to take care of the baby and that's her responsibility, and she feels bad, and that's why the storm is there'" (Kiefer, 64). At another reading, Kiefer recorded a spontaneous appraisal of *Outside* as a teacher read it to her class. The children tried to discern the significance of the lighted lantern in the cave. One wondered at the shadow it created. Another called the shadow pattern a "crack" and used this notion to explain how the ship at the bottom of the picture received light. Another viewer, though, believed this "crack" was actually a path, leading his or her classmate to link the picture's meaning to the title of the book, the path leading to "outside over there."

Kiefer's descriptions offer marvelous testimony to how excited and involved children can become in attempting to understand a picture book through both its intricate pictures and its elliptical text. Sendak's rhythmical interdependence of story and pictures calls on children's imaginative and analytic skills simultaneously.

Sendak has captured the attention of a wide-eyed audience of children because he constructs his picture books so carefully. The success of his pains as an artist reminds one of a scene from Tom Stoppard's play *The Real Thing.* In this play Annie asks Henry, a playwright, to edit a propaganda play written by a young revolutionary. Henry balks at the job when he sees the melodramatic, rough writing of the young man. Annie calls Henry a literary snob. "You're jealous of the idea of the writer," she challenges. "You want to keep it sacred, special, not something anybody can do."[17] At the height of their argument, Henry leaves the room and comes back carrying a cricket bat. He faces Annie with his defense:

Henry: Shut up and listen. This thing here, which looks like a wooden club, is actually several pieces of particular wood cunningly put together in a certain way so that the whole thing is sprung, like a dance floor. It's for hitting cricket balls with. If you get it right, the cricket ball will travel two hundred yards in four seconds, and all you've done is give it a knock like knocking the top off a bottle of stout, and it makes a noise like trout taking a fly . . . (*He clucks his tongue to make the noise*). What we're trying to do is to write cricket bats, so that when we throw up an idea and give it a little knock, it might . . . travel . . . (*He clucks his tongue again and picks up the script*). Now, what we've got here is a lump of wood of roughly the same shape trying to be a cricket bat, and if you hit a ball with it, the ball will travel about ten feet and you will drop the bat and dance about shouting "Ouch" with your hands stuck in your armpits. (Stoppard, 69–70)

Notes and References

Chapter One

1. "Acceptance Speech Andersen Award, 1970," *Bookbird* 8:2 (1970): 6; hereafter cited in text as "Andersen."

2. Selma G. Lanes, *The Art of Maurice Sendak* (New York: Harry N. Abrams, 1980), 26; hereafter cited in text.

3. *Caldecott & Co.: Notes on Books & Pictures* (New York: Michael di Capua/Farrar, Straus & Giroux, 1988), 213; hereafter cited in text as *C&C.*

4. Foreword to *R. O. Blechman,* by R. O. Blechman (New York: Hudson Hills Press, 1980), 8; hereafter cited in text as *Blechman.*

5. Muriel Harris, "Impressions of Sendak," *Elementary English* 48 (November 1971): 828; hereafter cited in text.

6. Walter Clemons, "The Grimm Reaper," *Newsweek,* 19 December 1988, 50; hereafter cited in text.

7. Philip Sendak, *In Grandpa's House,* trans. Semour Barofsky (New York: Harper & Row Junior Books, 1985); hereafter cited in text.

8. Ruth Krauss, *I'll Be You and You Be Me* (New York: Harper & Row, 1954); hereafter cited in text as *I'll Be You.*

9. *Outside Over There* (New York: Harper & Row, 1981); hereafter cited in text as *Outside.*

10. *In the Night Kitchen* (New York: Harper & Row, 1970); hereafter cited in text as *Night Kitchen.*

11. Martha Shirk, "Gloomy Relatives Inspired 'Wild Things' Author," *St. Louis Post-Dispatch,* 4 December 1989, 4; hereafter cited in text.

12. Charlotte Zolotow, *Mr. Rabbit and the Lovely Present* (New York: Harper & Row, 1962); hereafter cited in text as *Mr. Rabbit.*

13. *Where the Wild Things Are* (New York: Harper & Row, 1963); hereafter cited in text as *Wild Things.*

14. Justin Wintle, "Maurice Sendak," in *Pied Pipers: Interviews with the Influential Creators of Children's Literature,* ed. Justin Wintle and Emma Fisher (New York: Paddington, 1974), 21; hereafter cited in text.

15. Ruth Sawyer, *Maggie Rose: Her Birthday Christmas* (New York: Harper & Row, 1952).

16. Meindert DeJong, *Shadrach* (New York: Harper & Row, 1953); hereafter cited in text as *Shadrach.*

17. Meindert DeJong, *Hurry Home, Candy* (New York: Harper & Row, 1953); hereafter cited in text as *Candy.*

18. Anne Commire, ed., *Something about the Author* (Detroit: Gale Research, 1982), 27: 181; hereafter cited in text.

19. F.A.O. Schwarz, "The Ultimate Toy Catalogue 1988," pamphlet (New York: 1988), 1–2.

20. Marcel Ayme, *The Wonderful Farm* (New York: Harper & Row, 1951).

21. Ruth Krauss, *A Hole Is to Dig: A First Book of First Definitions* (New York: Harper & Row, 1952); hereafter cited in text as *Hole.*

22. Marcel Ayme, *The Magic Pictures* (New York: Harper & Row, 1954).

23. *Kenny's Window* (New York: Harper & Row, 1956); hereafter cited in text.

24. Sesyle Joslin, *What Do You Say, Dear?* (New York: Harper & Row, 1958).

25. *One Was Johnny* (New York: Harper & Row, 1962); hereafter cited in text.

26. *Higglety Pigglety Pop! or There Must Be More to Life* (New York: Harper & Row, 1967); hereafter cited in text as *Higglety Pigglety Pop!.*

27. *Very Far Away* (New York: Harper & Row, 1957); hereafter cited in text.

28. *The Sign on Rosie's Door* (New York: Harper & Row, 1960); hereafter cited in text as *Rosie's Door.*

29. *The Nutshell Library* (New York: Harper & Row, 1962); hereafter cited in text as *Nutshell.*

30. Quoted in Nat Hentoff, "Among the Wild Things," *New Yorker,* 22 January 1966, 66.

31. Bruno Bettelheim, "The Care and Feeding of Monsters," *Ladies' Home Journal,* March 1969, 48; hereafter cited in text.

32. Mary-Agnes Taylor, "In Defense of the Wild Things," *Horn Book Magazine,* December 1970, 642–46.

33. Bernard Holland, "The Paternal Pride of Maurice Sendak," *New York Times,* 8 November 1987, 42; hereafter cited in text.

34. Shelton L. Root, review of *In the Night Kitchen, Elementary English* 48 (February 1971): 262; hereafter cited in text.

35. David C. Davis, "Wrong Recipe Used *In the Night Kitchen,*" *Elementary English* 48 (November 1971): 860.

36. Lore Segel and Randall Jarrell, trans., *The Juniper Tree and*

Other Tales from Grimm (New York: Farrar, Straus & Giroux, 1973); hereafter cited in text as *Juniper Tree.*

37. Paul Heins, review of *The Juniper Tree, Horn Book Magazine,* April 1974, 136–38; hereafter cited in text.

38. Edgar Taylor, trans., *King Grisly-Beard: A Tale From the Brothers Grimm* (New York: Farrar, Straus & Giroux, 1973); hereafter cited in text as *Grisly-Beard.*

39. Frank Corsaro and Maurice Sendak, *The Love for Three Oranges* (New York: Farrar, Straus & Giroux, 1984), 9; hereafter cited in text as Corsaro.

40. John Cech, "Maurice Sendak: Off the Page," *Horn Book Magazine,* May–June 1986, 310; hereafter cited in text.

41. Mervyn Rothstein, "For Sendak, a Fairy Tale Is a Cause," *New York Times,* 19 October 1988, 13; hereafter cited in text.

42. Robert T. Jones, afterword to *The Cunning Little Vixen,* by Rudolf Tesnohlidek, trans. Tatiana Firkusny, Maritza Morgan, and Robert T. Jones (New York: Farrar, Straus & Giroux, 1985), 167; hereafter cited in text as Tesnohlidek.

43. Introduction to *Nutcracker,* by E. T. A. Hoffman, trans. Ralph Manheim (New York: Crown, 1984), ix; hereafter cited in text as *Nutcracker.*

44. Donnarae MacCann and Olga Richard, "Picture Books for Children," *Wilson Library Bulletin* 56 (September 1981): 49–50.

45. Joseph Nocera, "Publishing's High-Grade Hit Lit," *Newsweek,* 19 December 1988, 54; hereafter cited in text.

46. Wilhelm Grimm, *Dear Mili: An Old Tale by Wilhelm Grimm,* trans. Ralph Manheim (New York: Farrar, Straus & Giroux, 1988); hereafter cited in text as *Mili.*

47. Janet Adam Smith, "Not So Grimm," *New York Review of Books,* 24 November 1988, 24; hereafter cited in text.

48. Olive Ann Burns, "Boy Howdy, Ma'am, You Have Sent Us a Fine Book," *English Journal* 78 (December 1989): 19.

49. "Talk by Maurice Sendak Begins a Writers' Series," *New York Times,* 2 January 1989, 48.

50. "Appreciation," in *The Randolph Caldecott Treasury,* ed. Elizabeth T. Billington (New York: Frederick Warne, 1978), 14.

Chapter Two

1. "The Shape of Music," in *Readings about Children's Literature,* ed. Evelyn R. Robinson (New York: David McKay, 1966), 201; hereafter cited in text as "Shape of Music."

2. George Bodmer, "Ruth Krauss and Maurice Sendak's Early Illustrations," *Children's Literature Association Quarterly* 11 (Winter 1986–87): 181.

3. Ruth Krauss, *A Very Special House* (New York: Harper & Row, 1953), n.p.; hereafter cited in text as *Special House.*

4. Lynn Ward, "The Book Artist: Ideas and Techniques," in *Illustrators of Children's Books, 1946–1956,* ed. Ruth Hill Viguers, Marcia Dalphin, Bertha Mahony Miller (Boston: Horn Book, 1958), 32; hereafter cited in text.

5. Joseph H. Schwarcz, *Ways of the Illustrator: Visual Communication in Children's Literature* (Chicago: American Library Association, 1982), 24; hereafter cited in text.

6. James Smith Pierce, *From Abacus to Zeus: A Handbook of Art History,* 3d ed. (Englewood Cliffs, N.J.: Prentice Hall, 1987), 74.

7. Ruth Krauss, *Charlotte and the White Horse* (New York: Harper & Brothers, 1955), n.p.

8. Ruth Krauss, *Open House for Butterflies* (New York: Harper & Brothers, 1960), n.p.; hereafter cited in text as *Open House.*

9. John Gough, "The Unsung Dr. Seuss: Theo. Le Sieg," *Children's Literature Association* 11 (Winter 1986–87): 183.

10. Else Holmelund Minarik, *Little Bear* (New York: Harper & Row, 1957), 15; hereafter cited in text as *Little Bear.*

11. Else Holmelund Minarik, *Little Bear's Friend* (New York: Harper & Row, 1960), 62.

12. Else Holmelund Minarik, *A Kiss for Little Bear* (New York: Harper & Row, 1968), 18–21.

13. Perry Nodelman, *Words about Pictures: The Narrative Art of Children's Picture Books* (Athens: University of Georgia Press, 1988), 69; hereafter cited in text.

14. Meindert DeJong, *The Wheel on the School* (New York: Harper & Row, 1954), 6; hereafter cited in text as *Wheel.*

15. Meindert DeJong, *The House of Sixty Fathers* (New York: Harper & Row, 1956); hereafter cited in text as *Sixty.*

16. Geraldine DeLuca, "Progression through Contraries: The Triumph of the Spirit in the Work of Maurice Sendak," in *Triumphs of the Spirit in Children's Literature,* ed. Francelia Butler and Richard Rotert (Hamden, Conn.: Library Professional Publications, 1986), 147; hereafter cited in text.

Chapter Three

1. Maurice Sendak and Jonathan Cott, "A Dialogue with Maurice Sendak," in *Masterworks of Children's Literature: Victorian Color Picture*

Books, ed. Jonathan Cott (New York: Stonehill, 1983), 7:xix; hereafter cited in text as "Dialogue."

2. Geoffrey Summerfield, *Fantasy & Reason: Children's Literature in the Eighteenth Century* (London: Methuen, 1984), 230; hereafter cited in text.

3. Charles J. Fillmore, "The Case for Case," in *Universals in Linguistic Theory,* ed. Emmon Bach and Robert T. Harms (New York: Holt, Rinehart & Winston, 1968), 24; hereafter cited in text.

4. Bruno Bettelheim, *The Uses of Enchantment* (New York: Alfred Knopf, 1976), 127; hereafter cited in text.

5. Norma Bagnall, "What the Wild Things Are: Meaning through Linguistics," paper presented at the South Central Modern Language Association Conference, New Orleans, October 1980; hereafter cited in text.

Chapter Four

1. Ronald Paulson, *Emblem and Expression: Meaning in English Art of the Eighteenth Century* (Cambridge, Mass.: Harvard University Press, 1975), 14.

2. Charles Dickens, *Bleak House* (1853; reprint, London: Oxford University Press, 1948), 547; hereafter cited in text.

3. For this explication, I am indebted to the excellent study by Michael Steig, *Dickens and Phiz* (Bloomington: Indiana University Press, 1978), 143–46.

4. Mary-Agnes Taylor, "Which Way to Castle Yonder?" *Children's Literature Association Quarterly* 12 (Fall 1987): 142; hereafter cited in text.

5. Robert J. Kloss, "Fantasy and Fear in the Work of Maurice Sendak," *Psychoanalytic Review* 76 (Winter 1989): 575; hereafter cited in text.

6. Patricia Crown, interview, University of Missouri–Columbia, 17 April 1990; hereafter cited in text.

7. As quoted from *Mother Goose: The Original Volland Edition,* ed. Eulalie Osgood Grover (New York: Derrydale, 1984), n.p.; Sendak quotes this same introduction from *The Only True Mother Goose Melodies* in his essay "Mother Goose" (*C&C,* 18–19).

8. Richard E. Palmer, *Hermeneutics* (Evanston, Ill.: Northwestern University Press, 1969), 168.

9. Samuel Enoch Stumpfs, "Existentialism," in his *Socrates to Sartre: A History of Philosophy* 2nd edition (McGraw-Hill: New York, 1975), 462–66.

Chapter Five

1. "Playground Person," *New Yorker,* 7 November 1988, 30; hereafter cited in text as "Playground."
2. Elizabeth Closs Traugott and Mary Louise Pratt, *Linguistics for Students of Literature* (New York: Harcourt Brace Jovanovich, 1980), 275; hereafter cited in text.
3. Walter J. Ong, S.J., "The Writer's Audience Is Always a Fiction," *PMLA* 90:1 (Jan. 1975): 13; hereafter cited in text.
4. Cornelia Meigs, Anne Thaxter Eaton, Elizabeth Nesbitt, Ruth Hill Viguers, eds., *A Critical History of Children's Literature* (1953; reprint, New York: Macmillan, 1969), 447.
5. Susan Stewart, *Nonsense: Aspects of Intertextuality in Folklore and Literature* (Baltimore, Md.: Johns Hopkins University Press, 1979), 161–63.
6. Geraldine DeLuca, "Exploring the Levels of Childhood," *Children's Literature* 12 (1984): 4; hereafter cited in text.
7. Wayne Booth, *The Rhetoric of Fiction* (Chicago: University of Chicago Press, 1961), 300–9.
8. "Picture Book Genesis: A Conversation with Maurice Sendak," in *Proceedings of the Fifth Annual Conference of the Children's Literature Association,* (Villanova, Pa.: Villanova University, 1978), 5:31.
9. William F. Touponce, "The Journey as Cosmic Reverie: A Reading of Maurice Sendak's *In the Night Kitchen,*" in *Proceedings of the Thirteenth Annual Conference of the Children's Literature Association,* ed. Susan R. Gannon and Ruth Anne Thompson (Kansas City: University of Missouri–Kansas City, 1978), 92–95.
10. Carolyn Horovitz, "Fiction and the Paradox of Play," *Wilson Library Bulletin* 44 (December 1969): 397.

Chapter Six

1. William Wordsworth, "Preface to Lyrical Ballads," in *William Wordsworth: Selected Poems and Prefaces,* ed. Jack Stillinger (Boston: Houghton Mifflin, 1965), 448; hereafter cited in text.
2. Laurence Perrine, *Sound and Sense,* 5th ed. (1956; reprint, New York: Harcourt Brace Jovanovich, 1977), 361.
3. Karl Shapiro and Robert Beum, *A Prosody Handbook* (New York: Harper & Row, 1965), 6.
4. William Blake, *Songs of Innocence and of Experience: Shewing the Two Contrary States of the Human Soul,* in *The Complete Poetry and Prose of William Blake,* ed. David V. Erdman (Berkeley and Los Angeles: University of California Press, 1982), 7–32; hereafter cited in text.

5. James Holt McGraven, Jr., "'The Children Sport upon the Shore': Romantic Vision in Two Twentieth-Century Picture Books," *Children's Literature Association Quarterly* 11 (Winter 1986–87): 172.

Chapter Seven

1. Megan Anderson Bergstrom, *"Dear Mili,"* *Mothering,* Spring 1990, 52–53; hereafter cited in text.

2. Jane Doonan, *"Outside Over There:* A Journey in Style Part One," *Signal* 50 (May 1986): 92–103; hereafter cited in text. In her source study precedent to this one, Doonan points out that Sendak is aware of Runge's private meanings for his art, noting that Sendak read Robert Rosenblum's *Modern Painting and the Northern Romantic Tradition* while working on *Outside* and acknowledged that it "gave his own work great impetus" (94).

3. Rudolf M. Bisanz, *German Romanticism and Philipp Otto Runge: A Study in Nineteenth-Century Art Theory and Iconography* (Dekalb: Northern Illinois University Press, 1970), 20; hereafter cited in text.

4. J. B. C. Grundy, *Tieck and Runge: A Study in the Relationship of Literature and Art in the Romantic Period with Special Reference to "Franz Sternbald"* (Strasburg, Germany: Heitz, 1930), 75–76; hereafter cited in text.

5. Robert Rosenblum, *Modern Painting and the Northern Romantic Tradition: Friedrich to Rothko* (New York: Harper & Row, 1975), 65–66; hereafter cited in text.

6. Hanna Hohl, "Kunst und Liebe: Die Lehrstunde der Nachtigall," in *Runge in seiner Zeit* (Hamburg, Germany: Prestel-Verlag Munchen und Hamburger Kunsthalle, 1977), 163; hereafter cited in text. My thanks to William Rasch of Indiana University for translating Hohl's discussion from German into English.

7. Sendak's preliminary sketch for this illustration first accompanied Edwin McDowell's article "A Fairy Tale by Grimm Comes to Light" for the *New York Times* (28 September 1983, 1). In that sketch Sendak more closely quotes Runge's composition of the forest. In both drawings, a large oak tree rises on the left and a large evergreen on the right to frame the scene. As in Runge's composition, Sendak's focal point is dead center and lighted. Initially, Sendak's major alteration was that he peopled his scene with Mili and her mother instead of Runge's nursery of cupids and harp-playing poet.

8. It is interesting to note that in his own life Sendak first experienced the ramifications of the Holocaust when he was about the same age as Mili. In 1941, the day of his own rite of passage into adulthood,

his bar mitzvah, Sendak learned that his paternal grandfather had died in Europe. In the ensuing years, none of his father's family abroad would escape the Jewish persecution (Lanes, 23).

9. Smith interprets the identity of these characters in the context of Mili's century. She questions whether the characters on the bridge might be "peasants, also escaping from the Thirty Years' War?" (24).

10. John Canaday, "Early Classicism and Romanticism: England, Germany, and America," in *Mainstreams of Modern Art* 2nd ed. (New York: Holt, Rinehart and Winston, 1981): 35.

11. John Warren Stewig, "Kinds of Folk Literature," in his *Children and Literature,* 2d ed. (Boston: Houghton Mifflin, 1988), 210; hereafter cited in text.

12. "About the Author," preface to *The Griffin and the Minor Canon,* by Frank Stockton (New York: Harper & Row, 1963), 5; hereafter cited in text as "About."

Chapter Eight

1. Jonathan Cott, "Maurice Sendak: King of All Wild Things," *Rolling Stone,* 30 December 1976, 48–59; hereafter cited in text.

2. Jill P. May, "The Art of Victorian Books" (review of Jonathan Cott, ed., *Masterworks of Children's Literature: Victorian Color Picture Books*), *Children's Literature Association Quarterly* 13 (Spring 1988): 39.

3. Quoted in Saul Braun, "Sendak Raises the Shade on Childhood," *New York Times Magazine,* 7 June 1970, 40; hereafter cited in text.

4. William Anderson, "On Texts and Illustrators: Eight Books," *Children's Literature* 3 (1974): 214; hereafter cited in text.

5. Donnarae MacCann and Olga Richard, preface to their *The Child's First Books: A Critical Study of Pictures and Texts* (New York: H. W. Wilson, 1973), 2.

6. Mai J. Durham, "Some Thoughts about Picture Books," *Horn Book Magazine,* October 1963, 476–84; hereafter cited in text.

7. Horst Kunnemann, "A + B and Then What?" *Bookbird,* 8, No. 2 (1970): 65–70; hereafter cited in text.

8. Anne Commire, ed., *Something about the Author* (Detroit: Gale Research, 1983) 32: 133.

9. Paul G. Arakelian, "Text and Illustration: A Stylistic Analysis of Books by Sendak and Mayer," *Children's Literature Association Quarterly* 10 (Fall 1985): 122–27; hereafter cited in text.

10. "Maurice Sendak," *St. Louis Post-Dispatch* 12 October 1990, 6A, col. 1.

11. "Maurice Sendak Doctor of Fine Arts," *Horn Book Magazine,* August 1984, 515.

12. Adele Sarkissian, *Something about the Author Autobiography Series* (Detroit: Gale Research, 1987), 3:302; hereafter cited in text.

13. Anne Commire, ed., *Something about the Author* (Detroit: Gale Research, 1987) 49: 94; hereafter cited in text.

14. Stephen Schaefer, "An Open-Line to Childhood," *USA Weekend,* 7–9 November 1986, 6.

15. "Where the Wild Things Began," *New York Times Book Review,* 17 May 1987, 48.

16. Barbara Z. Kiefer, "The Child and the Picture Book: Creating Live Circuits," *Children's Literature Association Quarterly* 11 (Summer 1986): 63–68; hereafter cited in text.

17. Tom Stoppard, *The Real Thing* (Boston: Faber & Faber, 1982), 68; hereafter cited in text.

Selected Bibliography

Primary Works

Books

Hector Protector and As I Went Over the Water. New York: Harper & Row, 1965.

Higglety Pigglety Pop! or There Must Be More to Life. New York: Harper & Row, 1967.

In the Night Kitchen. New York: Harper & Row, 1970.

Kenny's Window. New York: Harper & Row, 1956.

The Love for Three Oranges. Written with Frank Corsaro. New York: Farrar, Straus & Giroux, 1984.

The Nutshell Library: Alligators All Around, Chicken Soup with Rice, One Was Johnny, and *Pierre.* New York: Harper & Row, 1962.

Outside Over There. New York: Harper & Row, 1981.

Pictures by Maurice Sendak. New York: Harper & Row, 1971.

Seven Little Monsters. New York: Harper & Row, 1976.

The Sign on Rosie's Door. New York: Harper & Row, 1960.

Some Swell Pup, or Are You Sure You Want a Dog? Written with Matthew Margolis. New York: Farrar, Straus & Giroux, 1976.

Very Far Away. New York: Harper & Row, 1957.

Where the Wild Things Are. New York: Harper & Row, 1963.

Illustrations for Others' Books

Along Came a Dog, by Meindert DeJong. New York: Harper & Row, 1958.

The Animal Family, by Randall Jarrell. New York: Pantheon, 1965.

Atomics for the Millions, by Maxwell Leigh Eidinoff and Hyman Ruchlis, introd. by Harold C. Urey. New York: McGraw Hill, 1947.

The Bat-Poet, by Randall Jarrell. New York: Macmillan, 1964.

The Bee-Man of Orn, by Frank Stockton. New York: Holt, Rinehart & Winston, 1964.

The Birthday Party, by Ruth Krauss. New York: Harper & Row, 1957.

Charlotte and the White Horse, by Ruth Krauss. New York: Harper & Row, 1955.

Circus Girl, by Jack Sendak. New York: Harper & Row, 1957.

The Cunning Little Vixen, by Rudolf Tesnohlidek. Translated by Tatiana Firkusny, Maritza Morgan, and Robert T. Jones. New York: Farrar, Straus & Giroux, 1985.

Dear Mili, by Wilhelm Grimm. Translated by Ralph Manheim. New York: Farrar, Straus, & Giroux, 1988.

Dwarf Long-Nose, by Wilhelm Hauff. Translated by Doris Orgel. New York: Random House, 1960.

Father Bear Comes Home, by Else Holmelund Minarik. New York: Harper & Row, 1959.

Fly by Night, by Randall Jarrell. New York: Farrar, Straus & Giroux, 1976.

The Giant Story, by Beatrice de Regnier. New York: Harper & Row, 1953.

The Golden Key, by George MacDonald. New York: Farrar, Straus & Giroux, 1967.

The Griffin and the Minor Canon, by Frank R. Stockton. New York: Harper & Row, 1963.

The Happy Rain, by Jack Sendak. New York: Harper & Row, 1956.

A Hole Is to Dig: A First Book of First Definitions, by Ruth Krauss. New York: Harper & Row, 1952.

The House of Sixty Fathers, by Meindert DeJong. New York: Harper & Row, 1956.

How Little Lori Visited Times Square, by Amos Vogel. New York: Harper & Row, 1963.

Hurry Home, Candy, by Meindert DeJong. New York: Harper & Row, 1953.

I'll Be You and You Be Me, by Ruth Krauss. New York: Harper & Row, 1954.

In Grandpa's House, by Philip Sendak. Translated by Semour Barofsky. New York: Harper & Row Junior Books, 1985.

I Want to Paint My Bathroom Blue, by Ruth Krauss. New York: Harper & Row, 1956.

The Juniper Tree and Other Tales from Grimm. Translated by Lore Segel and Randall Jarrell. New York: Farrar, Straus & Giroux, 1973.

King Grisly-Beard: A Tale from the Brothers Grimm. Translated by Edgar Taylor. New York: Farrar, Straus & Giroux, 1973.

A Kiss for Little Bear, by Else Holmelund Minarik. New York: Harper & Row, 1968.

Let's Be Enemies, by Janice May Udry. New York: Harper & Row, 1961.

The Light Princess, by George MacDonald. New York: Farrar, Straus & Giroux, 1969.

Little Bear, by Else Holmelund Minarik. New York: Harper & Row, 1957.

Little Bear's Friend, by Else Holmelund Minarik. New York: Harper & Row, 1960.

Little Bear's Visit, by Else Holmelund Minarik. New York: Harper & Row, 1961.

The Little Cow and the Turtle, by Meindert DeJong. New York: Harper & Row, 1955.

Lullabies and Night Songs. Edited by William Engvick. Music by Alec Wilder. New York: Harper & Row, 1965.

Maggie Rose: Her Birthday Christmas, by Ruth Sawyer. New York: Harper & Row, 1952.

The Magic Pictures, by Marcel Ayme. New York: Harper & Row, 1954.

The Moon Jumpers, by Janice May Udry. New York: Harper & Row, 1959.

Mr. Rabbit and the Lovely Present, by Charlotte Zolotow. New York: Harper & Row, 1962.

Nikolenka's Childhood, by Leo Tolstoy. New York: Pantheon, 1963.

No Fighting, No Biting!, by Else Holmelund Minarik. New York: Harper & Row, 1958.

Nutcracker, by E. T. A. Hoffmann. Translated by Ralph Manheim. New York: Crown, 1984.

Open House for Butterflies, by Ruth Krauss. New York: Harper & Row, 1960.

The Pleasant Fieldmouse, by Jan Wahl. New York: Harper & Row, 1964.

Sarah's Room, by Doris Orgel. New York: Harper & Row, 1963.

Schoolmaster Whackwell's Wonderful Sons, by Clemens Brentano. Translated by Doris Orgel. New York: Random House, 1962.

Seven Tales, by Hans Christian Andersen. New York: Harper & Row, 1959.

Shadrach, by Meindert DeJong. New York: Harper & Row, 1953.

She Loves Me, She Loves Me Not, Robert Keeshan. New York: Harper & Row, 1963.

The Singing Hill, by Meindert DeJong. New York: Harper & Row, 1962.

Somebody Else's Nut Tree and Other Tales from Children, by Ruth Krauss. New York: Harper & Row, 1958.

The Tale of Gockel, Hinkel and Gackeliah, by Clemens Brentano. Translated by Doris Orgel. New York: Random House, 1961.

A Very Special House, by Ruth Krauss. New York: Harper & Row, 1953.

What Can You Do with a Shoe?, by Beatrice de Regnier. New York: Harper & Row, 1955.

What Do You Do, Dear?, by Sesyle Joslin. New York: Harper & Row, 1961.

What Do you Say, Dear?, by Sesyle Joslin. New York: Harper & Row, 1958.

The Wheel on the School, by Meindert DeJong. New York: Harper & Row, 1954.

The Wonderful Farm, by Marcel Ayme. New York: Harper & Row, 1951.

Zlateh the Goat and Other Stories, by Isaac Bashevis Singer. Translated by Singer and Elizabeth Shub. New York: Harper & Row, 1966.

Essays

Caldecott & Co.: Notes on Books & Pictures. New York: Michael di Capua/ Farrar, Straus & Giroux, 1988.
"R. O. Blechman." Foreword to *R. O. Blechman,* by R. O. Blechman. New York: Hudson Hills, 1980.

Secondary Works

Books and Parts of Books

Bader, Barbara. "Maurice Sendak." In her *American Picture Books from Noah's Ark to the Beast Within,* 495–524. New York: Macmillan, 1976. Examines the eclecticism of Sendak's art, tracing his stylistic changes.
Commire, Anne, ed. "Maurice (Bernard) Sendak." In *Something About the Author,* 27:181–201. Detroit: Gale Research, 1982. Chronicles Sendak's life and works through 1981.
Cott, Jonathan, and Maurice Sendak. "A Dialogue with Maurice Sendak." In *Masterworks of Children's Literature: Victorian Color Picture Books,* Edited by Jonathan Cott, 7:ix–xxi. New York: Stonehill, 1983. Facsimiles with commentary for picture books by Caldecott, Crane, Greenaway, Potter, and others.
DeLuca, Geraldine. "Progression through Contraries: The Triumph of the Spirit in the Work of Maurice Sendak." In *Triumphs of the Spirit in Children's Literature,* Edited by Francelia Butler and Richard Rotert, 142–48. Hamden, Conn.: Library Professional Publications, 1986. Explores ambivalent vision of childhood throughout Sendak's works.
Jones, Dolores Blythe. "Maurice Sendak." In her *Children's Literature Awards and Winners: A Directory of Prizes, Authors, and Illustrators,* 1st. ed. supplement, 111. Detroit: Neal-Schuman, 1983. Chronicles Sendak's honors from 1967 to 1981.
Lanes, Selma G. *The Art of Maurice Sendak.* New York: Harry N. Abrams, 1980. An extensive, illustrated biography examining Sendak's life and canon.
Nodelman, Perry. *Words about Pictures: The Narrative Art of Children's*

Picture Books. Athens: University of Georgia Press, 1988. Examines in detail the dynamics between visual and verbal narrative using abundant examples, including many from Sendak.

Schwarcz, Joseph H. *Ways of the Illustrator: Visual Communication in Children's Literature.* Chicago: American Library Association, 1982. Examines how pictures express meaning in children's books.

Wintle, Justin. "Maurice Sendak." In *The Pied Pipers: Interviews with the influential creators of children's literature,* Edited by Justin Wintle and Emma Fisher, 20–34. New York: Paddington. Discusses Sendak's memories, influences, and motivations in his work.

Articles in Periodicals

Anderson, William. "On Texts and Illustrators: Eight Books." *Children's Literature* 3 (1974): 213–18. Reviews *Juniper Tree,* praising Sendak's choice of episodes and his animation, yet regretting the lack of "brooding malevolence" in the pictures (216).

Arakelian, Paul G. "Text and Illustration: A Stylistic Analysis of Books by Sendak and Mayer." *Children's Literature Association Quarterly* 10 (Fall 1985): 122–27. Compares *Wild Things* with *Nightmare in My Closet.*

Bell, Arthur. "An Affectionate Analysis of *Higglety Pigglety Pop!*" *Horn Book Magazine,* April 1968, 151–54. Review of *Higglety Pigglety, Pop!* focusing on narrative with brief examination of pictures' style.

Bergstrom, Megan Anderson. "*Dear Mili.*" *Mothering,* Spring 1990, 52–53. Reviews *Mili* as a disappointment among Sendak's canon.

Bettelheim, Bruno. "The Care and Feeding of Monsters." *Ladies' Home Journal,* March 1969, 48. Dialogue between psychoanalyst and mothers on dangers of *Wild Things.*

Bodmer, George R. "Ruth Krauss and Maurice Sendak's Early Illustration." *Children's Literature Association Quarterly* 11 (Winter 1986–87): 180–83. Examines the collaborative effort between Krauss and Sendak at the beginning of his career.

———. "The Pictured Story: Randall Jarrell by Maurice Sendak." *New Orleans Review* 15 (Summer 1988): 91–94. Examines collaborative effort between Jarrell and Sendak for *Bat-Poet, Animal Family,* and *Fly By Night.*

Braun, Saul. "Sendak Raises the Shade on Childhood." *New York Times Magazine,* 7 June 1970, 34–37, 40–54. Highlights the iconoclastic nature of Sendak's work.

Cech, John. "Maurice Sendak: Off the Page." *Horn Book Magazine,* May–June 1986, 305–13. Examines Sendak's later work in theater, film, music, and ballet, highlighting opera.

Clemons, Walter. "The Grimm Reaper." *Newsweek,* 19 December 1988, 50–52. Reviews *Mili* and *C&C,* highlighting the versatility of Sendak as an artist.

Davis, David C. "Wrong Recipe Used *In the Night Kitchen." Elementary English* 48 (November 1971): 856–64. Analyzes "the surface messages, implied messages, and the intricate mental process of comprehending messages" at play in *Night Kitchen* (860).

DeLuca, Geraldine. "Exploring Levels of Childhood: The Allegorical Sensibility of Maurice Sendak." *Children's Literature* 12 (1984): 3–24. Looks at Sendak's work as allegory, focusing on *Outside.*

Dohm, J. H. "Twentieth Century Illustrators: Maurice Sendak." *Junior Bookshelf* 30 (April 1966): 103–111. Argues that Sendak's style is far removed from Caldecott's.

Doonan, Jane. "'Outside over There': A Journey in Style Part One." *Signal* 50 (May 1986), 92–103. Explores the influence of the northern romantic tradition on *Outside.*

———. "'Outside over There': A Journey in Style Part Two." *Signal* 51 (September 1986): 172–87. Examines structure of Sendak's illustrations for *Outside* based on Alberti's geometric perspective.

Ford, Roger H. "Let the Wild Rumpus Start!" *Language Arts* 56 (April 1979): 386–93. Delineates the archetype of the "trickster" among Sendak's protagonists—Max, Hector, Jennie, Rosie, Pierre, and Mickey.

Heins, Ethel. *"Outside Over There" Horn Book Magazine,* June 1981, 288–89. Review favoring illustrations for *Outside* but criticizing the "slightly elliptical" narrative (288).

Heins, Paul. *"The Juniper Tree and Other Tales from Grimm." Horn Book Magazine,* April 1974, 136–38. Review of *Juniper Tree,* citing Sendak's borrowing from eclectic historical periods of art.

Hentoff, Nat. "Among the Wild Things." *New Yorker,* 22 January 1966, 39–73. Traces the reception of Sendak's work and discusses the influences on his art.

Kiefer, Barbara. "The Child and the Picture Book: Creating Live Circuits." *Children's Literature Association Quarterly* 11 (Summer 1986): 63–68. An ethnographic study of children's responses to picture books, including *Outside.*

Kloss, Robert J. "Fantasy and Fear in the Work of Maurice Sendak." *Psychoanalytic Review* 76 (Winter 1989): 567–79. Examines Sendak's transformation of "the psychoanalytic vision of experience into fiction and art" (578).

Kunnemann, Horst. "A + B and Then What?" *Bookbird* 8:2 (1970): 65–70. Contrasts pervasive, poor quality of contemporary picture books against 10 exemplary ones, including *Wild Things.*

Lanes, Selma G. "A Second Look: *Kenny's Window." Horn Book Magazine,*

March–April 1987, 192–95. Examines the foreshadowing in *Kenny's Window* of Sendak's other work.

MacCann, Donnarae, and Olga Richard. "Picture Books for Children." *Wilson Library Bulletin* 56 (September 1981): 49–51. Unfavorable review of Sendak's narrative and pictorial style for *Outside*.

McDowell, Edwin. "A Fairy Tale by Grimm Comes to Light." *New York Times,* 28 September 1983, 1, 26. Announces the discovery of Grimm's *Mili* and Sendak's plans for its illustration.

McGraven, James Holt, Jr. "'The Children Sport upon the Shore': Romantic Vision in Two Twentieth-Century Picture Books." *Children's Literature Association Quarterly* 11 (Winter 1986–87): 170–75. Examines the influences of Blake and Wordsworth present in *Wild Things* and McCloskey's *Time of Wonder* (1957).

Martin, C. M. "Wild Things." *Junior Bookshelf* 31 (December 1967): 359–63. Prophesies popular reception in Britain of *Wild Things* because of its cathartic nature.

Moseley, Ann. "The Journey through the 'Space in the Text' to *Where the Wild Things Are*." *Children's Literature in Education* 19 (Summer 1988): 86–93. Linguistical reading of *Wild Things* that notes codes for space in the text and for time in the pictures.

Reed, Michael D. "The Female Oedipal Complex in Maurice Sendak's *Outside Over There*." *Children's Literature Association Quarterly* 11 (Winter 1986–87): 176–80. Applies the psychoanalytic theory of a female oedipal fantasy to Ida's experience in *Outside*.

Root, Shelton L. "*In the Night Kitchen*." *Elementary English* 48 (February 1971): 262–63. Review of *Night Kitchen* that finds it unsuitable for young children.

Rothstein, Mervyn. "For Sendak, a Fairy Tale Is a Cause." *New York Times,* 19 October 1988, 13, 16. Review of *Mili,* emphasizing theme of death.

Shirk, Martha. "Gloomy Relatives Inspired 'Wild Things.'" *St. Louis Post-Dispatch,* 4 December 1989, 1, 4. Biographical excerpts from Sendak's address at Washington University.

Smith, Janet Adam. "Not So Grimm." *New York Review of Books,* 24 November 1988, 24, 26. Review of *Mili,* comparing it unfavorably with *Juniper Tree*.

Steig, Michael. "Reading *Outside Over There*." *Children's Literature* 13 (1985): 139–53. A source study of *Outside,* citing influences of George MacDonald's stories and Arthur Hughes's illustrations.

Taylor, Mary-Agnes. "In Defense of the Wild Things." *Horn Book Magazine,* December 1970, 642–46. A rebuttal to Bettelheim's pronouncements in 1969 against *Wild Things*.

———. "Which Way to Castle Yonder?" *Children's Literature Association Quarterly* 12 (Fall 1987): 142–44. Explores prevalent interpretations by students of *Higglety Pigglety Pop!* as an allegory about either life or death.

Touponce, William F. "The Journey as Cosmic Reverie: A Reading of Maurice Sendak's *In the Night Kitchen.*" In *Proceedings of the Thirteenth Annual Conference of The Children's Literature Association,* Edited by Susan R. Gannon and Ruth Anne Thompson, 92–95. Kansas City: University of Missouri–Kansas City.

White, David E. "A Conversation with Maurice Sendak." *Horn Book Magazine,* April 1980, 145–55. Discusses Sendak's divergence from picture books into opera libretto, theater production, and stage design.

Index

The Author

Amy Sonheim received her B.A. from Wheaton College and M.A. from Baylor University, both in English literature. She is pursuing nineteenth-century studies at the University of Missouri–Columbia.

The Editor

Ruth K. MacDonald is a professor of English and head of the Department of English and Philosophy at Purdue University. She received her B.A. and M.A. in English from the University of Connecticut, her Ph.D. in English from Rutgers University, and her M.B.A. from the University of Texas at El Paso. To Twayne's United States and English Authors series she had contributed the volumes on Louisa May Alcott, Beatrix Potter, and Dr. Seuss. She is the author of *Literature for Children in England and America, 1646–1774* (1982).